Lord, It's Time for Just You and Me, a Devotional by Cheryl Lynn Betz

"Cheryl Betz is a devoted student and teacher of the Scriptures who God has gifted in the writing of **Lord, It's Time for Just You and Me** (Volumes I, II, and III) to help us experience the joy and peace that comes from Devotional and Mediation time with God."

—Bill Baird, III,
Elder, First Presbyterian Church, Pikeville, Kentucky

"I was gifted Cheryl's first devotional *Lord, It's Time for Just You and Me*. Her stories, choice of Scriptures and prayers have had such a positive impact on my life. I have since bought her second devotional and have been able to share it with others. Her words and stories have made it easier to help make Godly decisions that we all wrestle with as young wives and mothers. God has used her to be a blessing to all who read her wonderful book."

—Allison Cooper,
Young wife and mother

"The everyday ups and downs of life can be difficult to handle. *Lord, It's Time for Just You and Me* is kept within my arm's reach daily. The relatable stories, Scripture readings and prayers so often give me what I need to have a Christ-centered day. It's a blessing in my life."

—Linda Lepore,
Retired Director of Development of a Non-Profit Company

"I believe this book is an invitation to develop an open, candid and honest relationship with your best friend—Jesus. You are invited into His presence in a similar way Cheryl uses to introduce and engage friends with one another—engaging, warm, honest and loving. You will see Cheryl and Jesus together in a friendship that will draw you to Him in a remarkable and intimate way."

—Rosemary W. Lukens,
RN, MA, Moderator, Evangelical Presbyterian Church

"When I pick up this sweet devotional, *Lord, It's Time for Just You and Me,* the title itself sets the stage for focus on God, and reminds me to let the competing intrusions of life fade into the background. Cheryl speaks with great insight and simplicity as she shares personal stories through which she's learned Biblical truths. I'm looking forward to more touching tales from the wellspring of her life experiences."

—**Robyn Phillips-Madson, DO, MPH;**
Assistant Professor of Family Medicine

"Cheryl writes this devotional in down-to-earth, easy-to-understand language that inspires her readers to want to live the way the Lord wants us to live. Her use of Scripture makes it relevant to our lives in a fresh way. *Lord, It's Time for Just You and Me* was a blessing to read."

—**Judi Patton,**
Former First Lady of Kentucky

"Cheryl Betz's devotionals have been an inspiration to me. Her eloquent way of delivering a Scripture passage, a practical way to live out that passage in my daily life, and a plan of action, have led me closer to my relationship with the Holy Spirit. They have helped push me further in my spiritual journey. I highly recommend her devotionals as support in your growth as you walk with Christ."

—**Mary Reilly,**
Cheryl's sister in Christ

BOOK 4

Lord, IT'S TIME FOR JUST You AND Me

A DEVOTIONAL BY

Cheryl Lynn Betz

LUCIDBOOKS

Lord, It's Time for Just You and Me, Book 4
A Devotional
Copyright © 2025 by Cheryl Lynn Betz

Published by Lucid Books in Houston, TX
www.LucidBooks.com

All rights reserved. No part of this publication may be reproduced, stored in a retrieval system, or transmitted in any form by any means, electronic, mechanical, photocopy, recording, or otherwise, without the prior permission of the publisher or Cheryl Lynn Betz, except as provided by USA copyright law.

All Scripture quotations, unless otherwise indicated, are taken from The Holy Bible, New International Version®, NIV®. Copyright ©1973, 1978, 1984, 1986, 2011 by Biblica, Inc.™ Used by permission of Zondervan. All rights reserved worldwide. www.zondervan.com The "NIV" and "New International Version" are trademarks registered in the United States Patent and Trademark Office by Biblica, Inc.™

Scripture quotations marked (ESV) are taken from the ESV® Bible (The Holy Bible, English Standard Version®), copyright © 2001 by Crossway, a publishing ministry of Good News Publishers. Used by permission. All rights reserved.

Scriptures quoted from The Holy Bible, New Century Version, copyright © 1987, 1988, 1991 by Word Publishing, Nashville, Tennessee 37214. Used by permission.

Scripture quotations marked (NKJV) are taken from the New King James Version®. Copyright © 1982 by Thomas Nelson. Used by permission. All rights reserved.

Scripture quotations marked (NLT) are taken from the Holy Bible, New Living Translation, copyright ©1996, 2004, 2015 by Tyndale House Foundation. Used by permission of Tyndale House Publishers, Carol Stream, Illinois 60188. All rights reserved.

Scripture quotations marked (RSV) are taken from The Revised Standard Version of the Bible, copyright © 1946, Old Testament section copyright © 1952 by the Division of Christian Education of the National Council of the Churches of Christ in the United States of America and are used by permission. All rights reserved.

Scripture quotations marked (TLB) are taken from The Living Bible copyright © 1971. Used by permission of Tyndale House Publishers, a Division of Tyndale House Ministries, Carol Stream, Illinois 60188. All rights reserved.

Scripture quotations marked MSG are taken from THE MESSAGE, copyright © 1993, 2002, 2018 by Eugene H. Peterson. Used by permission of NavPress. All rights reserved. Represented by Tyndale House Publishers, a Division of Tyndale House Ministries.

eISBN: 978-1-63296-912-5
ISBN: 978-1-63296-911-8

Special Sales: Most Lucid Books titles are available in special quantity discounts. Custom imprinting or excerpting can also be done to fit special needs. Contact Lucid Books at Info@LucidBooks.com

This book is dedicated to my Lord, my family, my readers, and my beloved sisters- and brothers-in-Christ who love me, flawed that I am. I love you and thank God for you.

SPECIAL THANKS

No person can accomplish any literary work entirely on her own. There are many people who have contributed to getting this work to this point. I am grateful and thank God for each one.

First, I am grateful for my family: my husband, William T. Betz, D.O., who has not only fixed many dinners while I have been focused on writing but has supported me with each of my books. I thank God for our adult children: our daughter and son-in-law, Amy and Brian Casselberry; our son and daughter-in-law, the Reverend John M. Betz and Kristi Betz, MD PhD. They have tolerated my endless questions and requests for help as I wrote *Lord, It's Time for Just You and Me, Book 4*.

Next, I want to thank the many pastors who have served and are serving our Lord, and from whose instruction I have benefitted significantly. I thank the Lord for the Reverend Trent Casto, the Reverend Chris Voorhees, the Reverend Brent Whitefield, the Reverend Chuck L. Betters, the Reverend Greg Blosser, the Reverend Bradley C. Smart, the Reverend Alistair Begg, and the late Reverend Charles Ashmore. Praise God for pastors who preach God's Word boldly and without apology.

My forever thanks go to Dr. Robyn Phillips-Madson who was one of the first to read my devotionals and to encourage me to pursue publishing them. I also want to thank my precious friend Vicki Jubanowsky for encouraging me greatly in my writing even to the point of helping me edit some of my works. I am abundantly blessed to count Bill Baird, Rosemary Lukens, Linda Lepore, Mary Reilly, and Pan Sanborn as more of my dear friends who continue to encourage me in my Christian walk. I want to add many thanks to my friend Pam Guilander and her daughter, Allison Guilander Cooper, who have opened the door for the Holy Spirit to use my work to bless their friends. What a blessing all these people are! All praise to God for giving me such extraordinary friends.

In addition, I want to thank the team at Lucid Books Publishing for their encouragement, their attention to detail, and their professional approach to publishing. I am grateful to have worked with them.

Even in naming all these people, I am sure there are those whom I have failed to name. I am so very grateful for the fact that as believers we are all part of Christ's body, and we serve Him together as He directs us (1 Corinthians 12:4–27).

Finally, let me conclude with this: I have no authority but that which the Lord has given me. I have no gifts but those which He has bestowed upon me. I have no life but that which He has breathed into me. And of course, I have no words but those which He has created. Thank You, Lord, for these gifts, and please, Lord, breathe life into these words to Your glory.

TABLE OF CONTENTS

    Letter to the Reader   xv

    Suggestions for Using This Devotional   xvii

1. Abide in Me   1
   a. Scripture Reading: John 15:4–11
   b. Scriptures Quoted: John 15:5
   c. Theme: As we abide in Christ, we will become who He wants us to be.

2. Be Prepared   5
   a. Scripture Reading: Luke 19:1–10
   b. Scriptures Quoted: 1 Peter 3:15
   c. Theme: We are always to be prepared to give an answer to our hope.

3. Be Thankful   9
   a. Scripture Reading: Colossians 3:15–17
   b. Scriptures Quoted: Psalm 118:1
   c. Theme: As God's children we have many reasons to be thankful.

4. Change   13
   a. Scripture Reading: Acts 10
   b. Scriptures Quoted: Acts 8:4; Acts 17:26
   c. Theme: The Lord allows and even directs changes in our lives.

5. Church Members and Church Participants   17
   a. Scripture Reading: Romans 12:6–8 and 1 Corinthians 12:4–11, 28
   b. Scriptures Quoted: Ephesians 4:11–12
   c. Theme: As church members we should be actively involved in helping the church ministry.

6. Clueless but Teachable   21
   a. Scripture Reading: Psalm 119
   b. Scriptures Quoted: Psalm 119:11
   c. Theme: Check all your work with the Bible.

7. Comparison   23
   a. Scripture Reading: Matthew 20:1–16
   b. Scriptures Quoted: Proverbs 14:30; Galatians 6:4–5
   c. Theme: Since God gives us all we need, we should not compare ourselves with others.

8. **Conversations with God**   27
   a. Scripture Reading: John 14:15–31
   b. Scriptures Quoted: Ephesians 6:18 and 1 Thessalonians 5:17
   c. Theme: We can have an ongoing conversation with God all day.

9. **Covet—You Shall Not**   33
   a. Scripture Reading: 1 Corinthians 12:4–31
   b. Scriptures Quoted: Deuteronomy 5:21
   c. Theme: Don't covet anything of any other person.

10. **Dropping Pansies**   37
    a. Scripture Reading: Luke 17:11–19
    b. Scriptures Quoted: Luke 17:17
    c. Theme: Let's live our lives showing our gratitude to all who serve us.

11. **Egypt after the Exodus**   39
    a. Scripture Reading: Exodus 3:1–14 and 5:1–5
    b. Scriptures Quoted: Exodus 12:31–32
    c. Theme: When the Israelites left Egypt, they left a significant void.

12. **Fear**   43
    a. Scripture Reading: Psalm 27
    b. Scriptures Quoted: Deuteronomy 10:12–13 and Isaiah 40:10
    c. Theme: There are healthy and unhealthy fears. Fearing God is a healthy fear.

13. **Feigned Interest**   47
    a. Scripture Reading: John 13:34–35
    b. Scriptures Quoted: 1 Samuel 16:7b
    c. Theme: We preach/teach/love and leave conversion to the Holy Spirit.

14. **A God Appointment**   51
    a. Scripture Reading: Acts 8:26–40
    b. Scriptures Quoted: Acts 17:26
    c. Theme: Our lives are full of God's appointments.

15. **God Healed Me**   55
    a. Scripture Reading: Isaiah 53:1–12
    b. Scriptures Quoted: 1 Peter 2:24
    c. Theme: God can heal anyone. But not everyone gets healed.

16. **God Healed My Husband**   59
    a. Scripture Reading: Acts 9:32–43
    b. Scriptures Quoted: Psalm 30:2; Psalm 103:2–3
    c. Theme: God sometimes healed through doctors' intervention.

17. God Is Not Done with You   63
   a. Scripture Reading: Philippians 1:18–26
   b. Scriptures Quoted: Psalm 90:12 and Jeremiah 29:11
   c. Theme: As long as we are alive, God will use us.

18. God, Our Creator   69
   a. Scripture Reading: Isaiah 45:18–25
   b. Scriptures Quoted: Psalm 24:1–2, Isaiah 37:16, and Acts 4:24
   c. Theme: God created everything and takes care of all He created.

19. God's Word—Truth   73
   a. Scripture Reading: 2 Timothy 3:14–17
   b. Scriptures Quoted: Psalm 24:1–2; Proverbs 4:20, 22; Isaiah 37:16
   c. Theme: Truth is found in God alone.

20. His Many Blessings   77
   a. Scripture Reading: Luke 17:11–19
   b. Scriptures Quoted: Deuteronomy 31:8
   c. Theme: God loves to bless His children—us.

21. Am a Sinner, Forgiven   81
   a. Scripture Reading: Romans 5:1–8
   b. Scriptures Quoted: Joshua 7:26
   c. Theme: God continues to work with us forgiven sinners.

22. An Influencer   85
   a. Scripture Reading: Revelation 20:11–15
   b. Scriptures Quoted: Jeremiah 29:11 and Isaiah 48:17
   c. Theme: We should be an influencer wherever God places us.

23. Jealousy   89
   a. Scripture Reading: Galatians 5:16–26
   b. Scriptures Quoted: Galatians 5:19–21a
   c. Theme: God made us just as He wants us to be, and we shouldn't be jealous of anyone.

24. Jellybeans   93
   a. Scripture Reading: Ephesians 1:18–22
   b. Scriptures Quoted: Ephesians 1:17
   c. Theme: We need to pray for candy stores instead of just for jellybeans.

25. Jennie   97
   a. Scripture Reading: James 2:1–4
   b. Scriptures Quoted: Colossians 3:12, 14
   c. Theme: Let God help you to put on love with each person you encounter every day.

26. **Jesus Is Saving a Seat for You**   101
    a. Scripture Reading: John 14:1–7
    b. Scriptures Quoted: Psalm 139:16
    c. Theme: You will always have a place with Jesus.

27. **Jonah**   103
    a. Scripture Reading: Jonah
    b. Scriptures Quoted: Psalm 145:8–9
    c. Theme: God works growth in the messenger and the audience.

28. **Judging**   107
    a. Scripture Reading: Matthew 7:1–5
    b. Scriptures Quoted: Matthew 7:4
    c. Theme: Be careful before you judge someone.

29. **The Lamb of God**   111
    a. Scripture Reading: Exodus 12
    b. Scriptures Quoted: John 1:29
    c. Theme: The Father's first announcement and introduction of His Son, the Lamb of God, was to shepherds who most likely raised sheep to be offered as sacrifices.

30. **Lazarus, Come Out!**   113
    a. Scripture Reading: John 11:17–44
    b. Scriptures Quoted: John 11:43b–44
    c. Theme: God calls all His children by name from death to eternal life.

31. **Life Preserver**   117
    a. Scripture Reading: John 14:15–31
    b. Scriptures Quoted: John 11:25–26
    c. Theme: Be ready and willing to share new life in Christ with anyone.

32. **The Majesty of God**   119
    a. Scripture Reading: Luke 9:37–43
    b. Scriptures Quoted: Luke 9:43
    c. Theme: God is majestic, and He created us in His image.

33. **Make the Call**   123
    a. Scripture Reading: 1 Samuel 18:1–4
    b. Scriptures Quoted: Proverbs 16:24
    c. Theme: Call a friend with whom you haven't spoken with for a while.

34. Mirrors   125
   a. Scripture Reading: Ephesians 4:22–24
   b. Scriptures Quoted: 2 Corinthians 3:18
   c. Theme: We can be mirrors that brightly reflect God's glory.

35. Mother   127
   a. Scripture Reading: Proverbs 31:10–31
   b. Scriptures Quoted: Galatians 5:22–31
   c. Theme: God answers prayers.

36. My Friend, Jan   131
   a. Scripture Reading: Psalm 1:1–3
   b. Scriptures Quoted: Mark 12:30–31
   c. Theme: The Jans in our lives remind us to let Christ's light shine through us.

37. On Call   135
   a. Scripture Reading: 1 Samuel 3:1–10
   b. Scriptures Quoted: Isaiah 6:8
   c. Theme: We want to be "on call" and ready for our Lord to use us.

38. Our New Life   137
   a. Scripture Reading: Acts 9:1–22
   b. Scriptures Quoted: Romans 12:2 and 2 Corinthians 3:17–18
   c. Theme: God will continue to change us until He calls us home.

39. Our Risen Lord   139
   a. Scripture Reading: Luke 24:1–50 and John 20:1–18
   b. Scriptures Quoted: 1 Corinthians 15:3–6
   c. Theme: Jesus saw His disciples and more than five hundred people after His resurrection.

40. The Parable of the Rich Farmer   143
   a. Scripture Reading: Luke 12:13–21
   b. Scriptures Quoted: 2 Chronicles 26:5b
   c. Theme: We need to submit all we are and all we have to the Lord for His use.

41. Perspective   147
   a. Scripture Reading: John 3
   b. Scriptures Quoted: Isaiah 43:1
   c. Theme: We need to make sure that our audience understands the words we use.

42. **Peter**   151
   a. Scripture Reading: Mark 16:1–7
   b. Scriptures Quoted: Mark 16:7
   c. Theme: When we confess our sin, God forgives us.

43. **The Proud Father**   155
   a. Scripture Reading: Psalm 139:1–18, 23–24
   b. Scriptures Quoted: Matthew 3:16–17
   c. Theme: The Father was proud of Jesus, and He is proud of us.

44. **Reflection**   161
   a. Scripture Reading: Ephesians 3:14–19
   b. Scriptures Quoted: John 3:16 and 1 John 3:1
   c. Theme: God loved us yesterday; He loves us now; and He will love us forever.

45. **Resist the Devil**   165
   a. Scripture Reading: Exodus 20:1–17
   b. Scriptures Quoted: James 4:7
   c. Theme: God promises us a way to escape temptation.

46. **The Rich Man**   169
   a. Scripture Reading: Mark 10:17–31
   b. Scriptures Quoted: Mark 10:17
   c. Theme: We must not place anyone or anything above God in priority.

47. **Scattering Seed**   173
   a. Scripture Reading: Matthew 13:1–23
   b. Scriptures Quoted: Mark 4:26–29
   c. Theme: With the Holy Spirit, we spread the Good News and let God produce the harvest.

48. **Seize the Idea!**   175
   a. Scripture Reading: Psalm 32:8–11 and 1 Samuel 3:1–10
   b. Scriptures Quoted: Psalm 16:7
   c. Theme: Write a note when God gives you a new idea.

49. **The Son Is Invading My Shade**   179
   a. Scripture Reading: Hebrews 12:1–11
   b. Scriptures Quoted: Psalm 139:23–24
   c. Theme: As long as we are here on this earth, our Lord will continue to refine us.

50. **The Stone Had Been Rolled Away** — 183
    a. Scripture Reading: Matthew 28:1–10
    b. Scriptures Quoted: John 20:19 and 26
    c. Theme: Jesus can bypass large stones, locked doors, anything.

51. **The Storm** — 187
    a. Scripture Reading: Mark 4:35–41
    b. Scriptures Quoted: Mark 4:38
    c. Theme: You can trust God to save you from storms.

52. **Thorns and Thistles** — 191
    a. Scripture Reading: Hebrews 5:11–6:8
    b. Scriptures Quoted: Hebrews 6:7–8
    c. Theme: Let God work with you to wash away the thorns and thistles in you.

53. **A Time to Wait** — 195
    a. Scripture Reading: Joshua 2
    b. Scriptures Quoted: 1 Kings 18:1
    c. Theme: Look for the good in times of waiting for our Lord.

54. **Tongues** — 201
    a. Scripture Reading: James 3:1–12
    b. Scriptures Quoted: Proverbs 18:21
    c. Theme: Use your tongue to bless people and God.

55. **Trust God's Grace** — 205
    a. Scripture Reading: Matthew 28:16–20
    b. Scriptures Quoted: 2 Corinthians 9:8
    c. Theme: Trust God to help you to tell others about Him and His love for them.

56. **The Truth** — 209
    a. Scripture Reading: 1 Kings 17:1–24
    b. Scriptures Quoted: 1 Kings 17:24
    c. Theme: Let's ask the Holy Spirit to give us discernment between truth and lies.

57. **The Veil of Unbelief** — 213
    a. Scripture Reading: Matthew 27:45–54
    b. Scriptures Quoted: 2 Corinthians 3:14
    c. Theme: Only God can lift the veil of unbelief.

58. **We Will Worship at His Feet** 217
    a. Scripture Reading: John 13:1–17 and Philippians 2:5–11
    b. Scriptures Quoted: Psalm 95:6 and Psalm 132:7
    c. Theme: When Christ returns, everyone will worship at His Feet.

59. **What Will You Say?** 221
    a. Scripture Reading: Luke 16:19–31
    b. Scriptures Quoted: Colossians 4:5–6 and 1 Peter 3:15–16
    c. Theme: We should always be ready to give reason for our hope, our faith in Christ.

60. **Wield Your Sword** 225
    a. Scripture Reading: Psalm 119:1–16
    b. Scriptures Quoted: Psalm 119:11 and Hebrews 4:12
    c. Theme: We all need to memorize Scripture.

Appendix I 229

Appendix II 231

Appendix III 237

LETTER TO THE READER

Thank you so very much for choosing this devotional! To those of you who have read Books 1, 2, or 3 of *Lord, It's Time for Just You and Me*, you will see that I have kept the same general layout in Book 4 as I used in my first three books. The content of this new book includes different stories and principles from those in my other books. I pray that you will use it as a method to grow in your faith and that He uses this offering to draw you closer to Him.

At the beginning of each devotional reading, I give two Scripture references. One is a brief verse or two printed at the top of the page for those frantic, on-the-run mornings, and the other gives the reference for a longer reading, which you can do when you have the time. God's Word is life and will give you so much more than any devotional filled with a man's or woman's words. How grateful I am that we have so many Bible translations available to us! I have found that a diet of reading His Word satisfies me as nothing else can.

Whether you are a new or mature Christian, I pray that the Holy Spirit will minister to you with His Word as you proceed through this devotional. I pray that as you spend time with Him, you will be blessed and become progressively more and more like Christ until you meet Him face to face. Let this be a time when you can sit before the Lord and say, "Lord, it's time for just You and me. Speak, for Your servant hears."

Enjoy and accept God's many blessings!

        Blessed in His service and His love,
        Cheryl Lynn Betz, a fellow work-in-progress

SUGGESTIONS FOR USING THIS DEVOTIONAL

Please allow me to offer a few suggestions that might enable you to glean optimal benefit as you use this book:

- **Block off a time each day** when you can sit before the Lord and say, "Okay, Lord, this is our time. It's just You and me." You can imagine that you are sitting in the chair on the cover of this book.
- **Pray each day before you begin to read.** Ask the Lord for a fresh word for the day. I love Psalm 119:18: *"Open my eyes to see wonderful things in your Word"* (TLB). This is my prayer for you. May the time you spend in this book and reading the Bible be profitable for the kingdom because it is time spent with our Lord.
- **Listen and believe.** Expect the Lord to speak to you each day. Expect the message to be pertinent to your life. Look for His direction, encouragement, instruction, and answers in the Scriptures and accompanying message provided in each reading. If you see no current relevance to your life, ask Him to reveal His message throughout the day. The author of the book of Hebrews makes an important observation in verse 2 of chapter 4: *"For we also have had the gospel preached to us, just as they did; but the message they heard was of no value to them, because those who heard did not combine it with faith."* I pray that as you read this book and God's Word you will *"combine it with faith."*

- **Use a Bible that you can understand** as you read the **Scripture Reading** at the beginning of each day. *Lord, It's Time for Just You and Me, Book 4* is a devotional, not a Bible study. Its function is to encourage you to spend time every day in fellowship with our Lord and enhance the time you spend with Him. If you are struggling with a version of the Bible that is hard to understand, your focus will be on the words rather than on the meaning. If the Bible is new to you, I recommend using the *Living Bible*, the *New Living Translation*, *The Message*, the *New International Version*, or the *New English Standard Version*. If you have a bookstore near you, look up each of these versions and see which of them is easiest for you to understand. These are reliable translations that are easier to understand than some of the other versions. If you would rather read the Bible on your smart phone, you can go to www.biblegateway.com. From there you can find the Scripture you want to look up in the Bible version you want to use. You will find NIV (*New International Version*), ESV (*English Standard Version*), NLT (*New Living Translation*), TLB (*The Living Bible*), MSG (*The Message*), and fifty-one more translations to choose from.
- This devotional is not a substitute for Bible study. I highly recommend that you seek out a Bible study in your church where you can study God's Word in depth. Usually, churches offer several Bible studies. Even in our small 350-member church in Kentucky, we offered a variety of Bible studies: one during the Sunday school hour for adults, one during the week for men, another for women, and one for teens. Look for a study that teaches the Bible from a spiritual rather than an academic view. Principally, the emphasis should be: What is the Lord saying in the Scriptures for me

today? What are the principles He wants me to learn, and how can I put them into practice? What are His promises on which I can stand in my everyday life?

- **This book is written by a human being, not God.** Therefore, it is possible that I have made mistakes. However, I have gone to great lengths to be sure of the accuracy of what I have written. I pray I have handled His Word correctly according to 2 Timothy 2:15.

- **Keep a devotional journal** where you can list the date of your specific prayer requests and leave space for the date upon which you receive an answer. This is also a good place to note specific, time-pertinent messages you receive from the Lord. You can keep track of questions that you have asked the Lord, such as, "Are You telling me to quit my job and move, or is this a diversion from the enemy?" Every time you believe He is talking to you about an issue, you can jot it down under your question. For example, before *Lord, It's Time for Just You and Me* existed, I was in a Christian bookstore looking for a devotional. I was disappointed in what was there, and I told God so. He very plainly said in my mind, "Then write your own!" Soon after that, He began to give me ideas, and now He's given me enough ideas to fill four books. Praise His holy name! Only with Him have I had anything to offer. He does speak to us today. We just need to listen.

- You will notice that in Appendix II, I have listed several Scriptures that pertain to the way the Lord faithfully leads us, step by step, showing us which way to go and how we can rely on Him to help us grow toward spiritual maturity. You may want to refer to these Scriptures on those days when your spiritual progress seems slow and you need some encouragement.

Let me send you forward with a promise from His Word and then a blessing. First, the promise is from Philippians 1:6: *"I am certain that God, who began the good work within you, will continue his work until it is finally finished on the day when Christ Jesus returns"* (NLT). Next is the blessing from Hebrews 13:20–21:

> *Now may the God of peace, who through the blood of the eternal covenant brought back from the dead our Lord Jesus, that great Shepherd of the sheep, equip you with everything good for doing his will, and may he work in us what is pleasing to him, through Jesus Christ, to whom be glory for ever and ever. Amen.*

ABIDE IN ME

Scripture Reading: John 15:4–11

"I am the vine; you are the branches. Whoever abides in me and I in him, he it is that bears much fruit, for apart from me you can do nothing" (John 15:5 ESV).

When our daughter-in-law was pregnant with our first grandson, our son would get close to Kristi's tummy and sing to the baby. While John was singing, the baby would move closer to his voice. Now that Kristi is pregnant again, both our son and our grandson sing to the baby in Kristi's tummy, and this baby also moves closer to the singing. Not only is this baby receiving nourishment from Kristi, but he's also enjoying entertainment from his dad and brother.

Just as John and Kristi's baby depends on Kristi to get nourishment, we depend on Christ to survive and grow. As the Scripture quoted above says, apart from Christ, we can do nothing. What does it mean *"to abide"*? It means to remain or to stay. Thus, we are to remain in Jesus. How do we do that? From the time we accepted Jesus as our Savior, we have had the Holy Spirit living in us, and we can go through our day talking with Him just as we would talk to our spouse, our children, our friends. He is our constant companion. When we go to Bible study or to play bridge or pickle ball, don't we greet our fellow players with a hug followed by either our asking how they are, or rejoicing in our being able to get together? We interact with them. We certainly don't ignore them. They are our friends. Don't we always have lots to say to one another? Why should we be any different with the Holy Spirit? We have lots of friends and acquaintances, but not all of them love us. The Holy Spirit loves us with His perfect love and is interested in our lives. Why would we not speak with Him and trust Him?

I recently heard a story about a man who said he could bowl a perfect game, and he knew he could do it while everyone watched. He proceeded to walk down the bowling lane until he was quite close to the pins. He rolled his bowling ball, and indeed, he did bowl a perfect game. Following that demonstration, he bowled another game while standing behind the foul line, the correct distance to the pins, but he did not bowl a perfect game. The closer he was to the pins the more accurately he was able to bowl, and the less likely he was to miss. Likewise, the closer we stay to our Lord, the better we can know Him and follow Him, and the less likely we are to miss His guidance.

Because we love our Lord, we want to stay close to Him, to remain with Him, to abide in Him. He loves us—the Father, the Son, and the Holy Spirit love us. Let's stay as close to Him as we can while we await His return when we will see Him face to face (1 Corinthians 13:12).

Plan of Action

1. Are you physically attending a Bible-believing church? Many of us live-streamed services during the COVID-19 shutdown. However, now we need to go back to worshiping in a church building, so we have that physical contact with other believers. We need reassurance that our sisters- and brothers-in-Christ can give us. We need fellowship with other Christians.

2. Are you in a Bible study? If not, I recommend that you find a good Bible-teaching study in your neighborhood or a Bible-believing study in your church. Spending time with other believers helps us to abide in Christ.

3. Just as we need Christian fellowship, the Lord wants us to participate socially with our neighbors. We are to be good citizens in our communities. Otherwise, how do we influence what laws we have, and how do we witness to unbelievers if we only surround ourselves with Christians? The Lord has gifted me to be an encourager to other believers. But He has also made it plain that I am to move in other circles in addition to those of my fellow Christian believers.

Prayer

My Lord and my God, I love You so much. I love Your Word, which You have graciously given to us to let us know how much You love us. It teaches us what You are doing, what You want us to do, and how You want us to behave. Please help us to be Your arms to love Your creation here on earth. Help us to shine with Your light to help other find You. Please keep us close to You always until we see You face to face. Thank You, Lord. I pray in my Savior Jesus' name. Amen.

BE PREPARED

Scripture Reading: Luke 19:1–10

"Always be prepared to give an answer to everyone who asks you to give a reason for the hope that you have. But do this with gentleness and respect" (1 Peter 3:15).

Did you think of the Boy Scouts when you read the title of this devotional? That is their motto. As Christians we, too, are to be prepared. And one of the ways we are to be prepared is to share our story of what we were like before Christ brought us into His Kingdom and how He has changed our life. Remember that the emphasis should be on Christ's changing us rather than going into dramatic detail of how bad we were in our Christ-less life. No one benefits from our going into intricate details about our before-Christ life. You may think that you will never have the opportunity to share how Christ saved your life. Therefore, let me tell you about one friend's experience which found him unprepared for the company he was blessed and surprised to have.

This friend is a wonderful, godly gentleman in our church. He said that he had gone to a gathering which he knew former Vice President Pence would also attend, but he never expected to meet him let alone have some private time with him. Yet near the end of the evening, he found himself alone with the former VP while he was waiting for his car. Our friend said that because he was totally unprepared, his mouth was running away with him as he tried to fill the quiet. He said that his mind was saying, "Shut up! Just shut up! You are just rambling on and on and on!" But he said that his mouth would not listen to his mind, and he continued to jabber. Our friend was unprepared.

Do you remember the story in Luke 19:1–10 about Zacchaeus who knew that Jesus was coming into his city, and he wanted to see Him. However, since he was very small, he climbed a tree to have a better look. *"When Jesus reached the spot, he looked up and said to him, 'Zacchaeus, come down immediately. I must stay at your house today'"* (Luke 19:5). Some day in your future, the Holy Spirit may say, "Donna" or "Susan" or "James, I am bringing someone to you today, and I need you to tell her your salvation story." I want you to be ready. I have written out my salvation story on my computer, and I am asking you to do the same either in a notebook or computer. Of course, you won't read it to the person God sends your way. But by writing it, you will have thought your story out.

As you write your story, include some appropriate Scriptures because God's Word is living, and it will give the listener a reference point. Also, we know that when we use His Word, it makes a difference to those who hear it. Isaiah 55:10–11 says:

> *As the rain and snow come down from heaven and do not return to it without watering the earth and making it bud and flourish . . . so is my word that goes out from my mouth: It will not return to me empty, but will accomplish what I desire and achieve the purpose for which I sent it.*

This is why we love to bless others with His Word. He blesses others as they hear it and read it, and He blesses us as we speak it. You may find Appendix I at the back of this book to be helpful as you think through your new life, born-again story (John 3:3). Please don't feel intimidated. God wants you to be prepared. Read again the quoted Scripture at the beginning of today's devotion. *"Always be prepared. . . ."* He loves you, and He loves the people with whom He wants you to share your story.

Let me add that just in case God opens an opportunity for you to share your story, He is faithful and will remind you of the things you need to say. Don't shy away because you haven't put it together in your head or on paper. If the Lord gives you the occasion, He will speak through you. You have only to ask Him.

Plan of Action

1. You have your homework set before you. Sit down and write what or who led you to confessing your sins and accepting Christ as your Savior. We know that *"the wages of sin is death"* (Romans 6:23). Both you and I should die because of our sin; but instead, we are given eternal life in Heaven with our God.

2. Be ready to tell your story. You might be surprised when the opportunity is placed before you. But you will be ready. ☺ Hurrah for you! Hurrah for God our Father, God the Son, and God the Holy Spirit!

Prayer

My Lord, I love how You prepare us and then give us a nudge to speak when we should. You are so generous with us! You let us bless others with Your Word, and You bless us with Your presence. I agree with Paul who wrote in Galatians 2:20 where he says, "I have been crucified with Christ and I no longer live, but Christ lives in me. The life I now live in the body, I live by faith in the Son of God, who loved me and gave himself for me." Use me whenever and wherever You desire, Lord. You know I am Yours. I pray in Jesus' beautiful and powerful name. Amen.

BE THANKFUL

Scripture Reading: Colossians 3:15–17

"Give thanks to the Lord, for he is good; his love endures forever" (Psalm 118:1).

I was recently in a Bible study where we were examining Colossians 3:15–17. At first view, it seemed easy to me because one of the verses that has directed my life for many years is verse 17: *"And whatever you do, whether in word or deed, do all in the name of the Lord Jesus, giving thanks to God the Father through him."*

What I had failed to notice before doing the study is that at the end of verse 15, 16, and 17, Paul, through the inspiration of the Holy Spirit, repeats the admonishment to be thankful. Robert Schuller was a former televangelist who had a gift of saying Scripture in a way that helped people remember. In reference to these verses, he might have said something you have probably heard before: "Have an attitude of gratitude."

In other Bible studies, our pastors and other leaders have taught us that when a word or idea is repeated in a sentence or paragraph in the Bible, God is calling special attention to those points. Three times in three consecutive verses, the Holy Spirit tells us to be thankful. Be thankful that you will *"let the peace of Christ rule in your heart"* (Colossians 3:15). Be thankful that you *"let the word of Christ dwell in you richly as you teach and admonish one another with all wisdom, and as you sing psalms, hymns, and spiritual songs"* (Colossians 3:16). Be thankful to God the Father through Christ, and in *"whatever you do, whether in word or deed, do it all in the name of the Lord Jesus"* (Colossians 3:17). Therefore, out of obedience to our Lord, we are and will be thankful.

Let's consider some of the reasons we should be thankful. First, He created us. *"For you created my inmost being; you knit me together in my mother's womb"* (Psalm 139:13). Our very breath comes from Him: *"He himself gives all men life and breath"* (Acts 17:25b). He gives us eternal life. *"For God so loved the world [that's us] that he gave his one and only Son [Jesus], that whoever believes him shall not perish but have eternal life"* (John 3:16). He walks with us throughout our life. *"You [God] both precede me and follow me, and lay your hand of blessing on my head"* (Psalm 139:5 TLB). As we go through life, He continues to work with us and change us to become more mature Christians: *"He who began a good work in you will carry it on to completion until the day of Christ Jesus"* (Philippians 1:6).

No matter what happens in our life, He will bring good out of it. *"And we know that in all things God works for the good of those who love him [that's you and me], who have been called according to his purpose [again, that's you and me]"* (Romans 8:28). Finally, let's be thankful that God has given us His Word to teach us and lead us. *"All Scripture is God-breathed and is useful for teaching, rebuking, correcting and training in righteousness, so that the man of God may be thoroughly equipped for every good work"* (2 Timothy 3:16–17). If you need additional incentive to thank God, read Psalms 118 and 138.

Plan of Action

1. If you are not in a Bible study, I recommend that you find one where you will read the Bible and not work primarily with someone's ideas or written works. In the "Suggestions for Using This Devotional" at the beginning of this book, I stated that this devotional is not a substitute for Bible study. Find a study that looks at the Bible from a spiritual rather than an academic point of view.

2. Thank God for your pastors and other church leaders, including your Bible study leader. From time to time, take a few minutes to write them a note letting them know that you are grateful for them.

Prayer

Lord, You are such a generous, loving God, and I do thank You for giving me life. I know that I am secure in Your care. I ask that You continue to establish an attitude of gratitude in me toward You and toward others. Thank You, Lord. I pray in the name of Jesus, my beloved Savior. Amen.

CHANGE

Scripture Reading: Acts 10

"Those who had been scattered preached the word wherever they went" (Acts 8:4).

"From one man he made every nation of men, that they should inhabit the whole earth; and he determined the times set for them and the exact places where they should live" (Acts 17:26).

Sometimes, the Lord introduces His children to new ways, new accents, new cultures. A few years ago, the Lord moved us from the Kansas City area, where we had lived all our lives, to Eastern Kentucky in the Appalachian Mountains. In this part of the United States, we heard new accents and were immersed into a new culture, both of which we grew to love. He led us to a wonderful church with precious people who also loved and served God.

Several years ago, I went on a short-term mission trip to Ecuador. The Lord surrounded my team with His followers. When we sang together in worship to Him, we rejoiced because even though we didn't speak the same language, we recognized the songs and the authentic love for our Lord. Yes, the language and the culture in Ecuador were different from ours, but it was a wonderful experience.

In the Scripture reading above, our Lord was preparing Peter to preach to a gathering of Gentiles. Without God's leading by giving him the three visions, Peter would not have gone because it was against the Jewish law to associate with or visit Gentiles. For Peter this experience would be a major change for him. But he obediently followed God's instruction and His good news was preached to a new group of people.

So often we tend to bristle at change. We like the familiar and look critically at something or someone new. But in each of the examples listed above, the changes were very good even though they were different. As Christians we need to stay fluid enough that we can move when God calls us to move. It might mean crossing the street to greet a new neighbor. It could mean that the Lord wants you to get involved in a neighborhood activity where you will meet new people. He might call you to invite someone new to your church or Bible study. We should not live our lives looking critically at change.

In Alistair Begg's *365 Daily Devotions,* he writes, "He shapes our minds, our morals, our manners, and our means so we can be brought under the control of the one whom we've declared as Majesty."[1] Moving His people from one city, state, or country to another is not a big deal to Him, and He will most certainly place us where we can best learn from Him and best serve Him to His glory.

As we welcome newcomers into our different circles, we can remember that we are not the first to have people from another culture who may have an accent, may even speak a different language from ours. When the Lord scattered the early believers

---

1. Alistair Begg, *Truth for Life, 365 Daily Devotions* (The Good Book Company, 2021), 138.

to different parts of the world, they were the newcomers entering foreign places, and they *"preached the word wherever they went"* (Acts 8:4). So even though they were in a new place, the Lord moved them to share the good news.

Plan of Action

1. When one of the teachers of the law asked Jesus which of the commandments was most important, Jesus answered, *"Love the Lord your God with all your heart and with all your soul and with all your mind. This is the first and greatest commandment. And the second is like it: Love your neighbor as yourself"* (Matthew 22:37–39). We are to love our literal neighbors, and we are to love neighbors that may not live next door to us, but they may be new to our neighborhood. Or they may be people the Lord places in our lives. Let's listen to our Lord to find out how He wants us to love our neighbor. Maybe we are supposed to make brownies and take them to their home, or perhaps we are to pray for them.

2. Let's be careful not to believe that someone is not as smart as we are just because of an accent or the way they dress or tattoos or piercings. God made every person on earth. Therefore, we should treat everyone we meet with that in mind.

Prayer

Lord, You told Samuel not to consider the outward appearance when he was looking for the king who would replace Saul (1 Samuel 16:7). You told Samuel that You look at the heart of a person. Help us to look beyond the outward appearance. Open our eyes to see the heart of a person. You have made everyone unique. Not bad, just different. Thank You for leading us and loving us. We pray in Jesus' name. Amen.

CHURCH MEMBERS AND CHURCH PARTICIPANTS

Scripture Reading: Romans 12:6–8 and 1 Corinthians 12:4–11, 28

"It was he [Christ] who gave some to be apostles, some to be prophets, some to be evangelists, and some to be pastors and teachers, to prepare God's people for works of service, so that the body of Christ may be built up" (Ephesians 4:11–12).

As you can tell from the title of this devotion, some church members are not always participants. One Sunday, our pastor began his sermon by asking us if we were actively involved in the ministry of our church. Had we volunteered to serve as an usher, or as a greeter, or as a Sunday School teacher, or some other role? If not, why not?! He explained that a church of our size (1500+ members) requires lots of help, and every one of us should be helping in some way.

Because our church is so large, during the six-week new members' class, each person is strongly encouraged to designate an area where he or she would like to help. We could choose from a long list of services. You may have heard that of all the members in a church, usually everything is handled by 15 percent of the members. Our leaders don't want that to be so in our church, and they actively recruit members for many of the ministries. For a while, my husband and I attended the worship and different activities, but we were just on the taking end. We were not actively helping our church. The Holy Spirit nudged us to give to our church by serving at the Welcome Desk. If you knew my husband, you would say, "Well of course you are welcoming people to your church! That is so Bill!" Yes, it is, and I love serving with him!

Are you a church member only? Or are you a church participant? Regardless of the size of the church, people are needed to fill many ministry spots. You may be a natural greeter who stands at the door and welcomes people into worship. You may be an exceptional proofreader who is needed to read over the many papers that flow in the church (bulletins, flyers, emails, ads, and such). Our Lord gives all His children gifts, which we are supposed to use to build up His church. The gifts He has given us are not just for our selfish use. If you are a church member, you have a gift that your church can use. Volunteer by contacting a church leader. You will be blessed just as your church will be blessed by your service. If you are already a church participant, you know what a special treat it is to serve your church body.

Plan of Action

1. Even if you don't know what your spiritual gift is, look over the different activities in your church. Which one interests you? Contact the leader and offer your help. Soon you will know if that is where you can be useful or not. If not, volunteer in another area such as summer Bible school or the choir.

2. Remember that as you find your spot, you will probably have to submit to someone who is the leader of that group. Rarely do we move into a group and automatically become the leader. Be a helper and not a critic.

3. If you are already a church participant and someone offers to help, graciously accept their offer if you need help. If you don't need help, perhaps you can point the person toward another area, which might need assistance.

Prayer

Lord, we are all part of Your body. Please help us to work together for Your glory. We are all sinners saved by grace to do good work. For those people who are not actively serving in one of Your churches, move them to become active. For those of us who are actively serving, help us to remember that we do everything in love to help build up, edify, and encourage Your body of believers all to Your glory and in Jesus' name. Amen.

> "Be devoted to one another in brotherly love. Honor one another above yourselves" (Romans 12:10).

CLUELESS BUT TEACHABLE

Scripture Reading: Psalm 119

"I have hidden your word in my heart that I might not sin against you" (Psalm 119:11).

Many years ago, I was a cheerleader in high school, but I didn't understand the game of football. At our first football game when our team had the ball, I started the cheer "Push 'em back! Push 'em back! Waaaay back!" Quickly our coach came over to us and stopped the cheer. He said to the cheerleaders, "Monday morning before school begins, we are having a meeting." He graciously taught us the fundamentals of football so when we cheered, we had some idea of what was happening on the field.

Just as I didn't understand football even though I still led the pep club in cheering, some writers of Christian songs, books, and other materials which may not be in line with Scripture. The tune may be catchy. The book may be interesting. The writer may be talented. The pastor may ooze charisma. But the message may not be in accord with Scripture. All kinds of media are directed and delivered by fallible human beings. Our God is perfect. We are not. It is our responsibility to check our ideas and work with God's word. Even with the best of intentions, there may be times when we let something slip by not realizing that it is our idea and not in agreement with God's word. James 3:1 warns: *"Not many of you should presume to be teachers, my brothers, because you know that we who teach will be judged more strictly."* Those of us who have the responsibility of delivering a Christian message need to scrutinize our work to see whether it is aligned with God's word. I love what Alistair Begg, a pastor in Cleveland, Ohio, often tells his congregation: "You are intelligent people. Look it up in your Bibles to see if what I am saying is true." As teachers we must check our messages and be sure we are accurately handling the word of God (2 Timothy 2:15).

Plan of Action

1. When reading books, listening to songs, or listening to pastors and teachers, ask the Lord to help you to discern whether the information is in line with His word. As I said before, since we are all human, there is the possibility of error. Most of the time, errors are made by mistake. Occasionally, lies are spoken intentionally; those people have to answer to God.

2. If you have the opportunity/blessing to teach a group, whether they are a Christian group or secular, ask God to put a guard over your mouth so you only teach what is true and honorable to Him. Depend on Psalm 32:8, which says, *"I will instruct you and teach you in the way you should go; I will counsel you and watch over you."* Constantly check your work with the Bible to be sure you are correct.

Prayer

Father, I always want to teach and speak truth. Please help me to honor You as I present Your word. And please, Lord, always help me to be teachable, all to Your glory. In Jesus' name I pray. Amen.

COMPARISON

Scripture Reading: Matthew 20:1-16

"A heart at peace gives life to the body, but envy rots the bones" (Proverbs 14:30).

"Each one should test his own actions. Then he can take pride in himself, without comparing himself to somebody else, for each one should carry his own load" (Galatians 6:4-5).

My husband and I were watching *The Voice*, which is a television program where people sing and compete until one person wins. As we were watching several of the singers perform together, we noticed that one of the contestants was much shorter than the others. However, when he was standing alone, we didn't notice that he was particularly short.

That reminded me of a sermon by one of my pastors many years ago. He said if we are looking at others and wanting what they have, that is having an ungrateful heart. In a sermon on the parable of the laborers in the vineyard (Matthew 20:1-16), he pointed out the mistake people make when they have comparing eyes. Comparisons can breed discontent and envy. Theodore Roosevelt reportedly said, "Comparison is the thief of joy."

As Christians we can rejoice that God made us just the way we are supposed to be. *"I praise you because I am fearfully and wonderfully made"* (Psalm 139:14). I find this truth gives me so much freedom from striving to please others by being what I think they expect me to be. Apostle Paul asserted his identity in Christ alone: *"Am I now trying to win the approval of men, or of God? Or am I trying to please men? If I were still trying to please men, I would not be a servant of Christ"* (Galatians 1:10). Yes, we want to serve God over others. God doesn't compare me to anyone else; He created me to be me, no one else. God created you to be you, no one else. Isn't that a marvelously freeing gift of God?

We find that He gives us the gifts that He wants us to have (Romans 12:4-8). He doesn't expect us to do anything that He hasn't already given us the gifts to accomplish His work, and He doesn't want us to do anyone else's job. He supplies us with all our needs (Philippians 4:19).

Our Lord has even placed us in the exact neighborhood where He wants us to live, where our gifts can best be used. *"From one man he made every nation of men, that they should inhabit the whole earth; and he determined the times set for them and the exact places where they should live"* (Acts 17:26). He has plans for us (Jeremiah 29:11). He wants His best for us (Romans 8:28). He loves us (John 3:16).

Plan of Action

1. Think through this last week. Was there a time when you compared what you had or who you are with someone else? Why did you make that comparison? Was it God urging you to enlarge your vision as to what you can accomplish with Him? Or was it envy or greed on your part?

2. Ask Him which it was: envy or greed or His expanding your vision. If the former, ask for forgiveness and ask Him to give you a grateful heart and mind. If the latter, ask Him what steps you are to take to make this vision reality.

Prayer

Lord, You are such a gracious and generous God. Please help us to be satisfied and thankful with where You have placed us, with the assets and friends You have given us, and with the family You have given us. Please open our eyes to see the vision You have for us. Help us to seek You and Your will for our lives every day. We love You, Lord, and we pray in Jesus' name. Amen.

CONVERSATIONS WITH GOD

Scripture Reading: John 14:15–31

"And pray in the Spirit on all occasions with all kinds of prayers and requests" (Ephesians 6:18).

"Pray continually" (1 Thessalonians 5:17).

Since, as Christians, we have the Holy Spirit living in us, how can we live and not pray continually? How can we be with the Spirit every second, every minute, every hour, every day of our lives and not speak to Him? If we live that way, I have to ask, "Do we really believe He is with us?" If we did, wouldn't we speak with Him? First Corinthians 6:19 reads *"Or do you not know that your body is a temple of the Holy Spirit within you, whom you have from God"* (ESV)? How would you feel if you spent twenty-four hours a day with someone, and they never spoke with you? I have heard it said, "To be a Christian without prayer is no more possible than to be alive without breathing." That paints the picture, doesn't it?

As Christians we have the honor of having the Creator of the universe, the One who can answer all our questions, living in us. We are told in Zephaniah 3:17, *"The LORD your God is with you, he is mighty to save. He will take great delight in you, he will quiet you with his love, he will rejoice over you with singing."* Our God takes great delight in us! Doesn't that Scripture bless your socks off? The God who created the heavens and the earth, the God who created butterflies, maple trees, oceans, prairies, and mountains takes great delight in us!

Before Christ came to this earth in the flesh, God spoke to people through His prophets; yet even the prophets did not have the privilege of having ongoing conversations with God every moment of every day. In John 14:16–17 Jesus explains to his disciples that when He leaves, He will not leave them alone:

> *I will ask the Father, and he will give you another Helper to be with you forever—the Spirit of truth. The world cannot accept him, because it does not see him or know him. But you know him, because he lives with you and he will be in you* (NCV).

Then in the same chapter, verse 20, Jesus continues with *"On that day you will realize that I am in my Father, and you are in me, and I am in you."* I will say it again. We are blessed to have the Creator of the universe abiding in us—the Holy Spirit. Doesn't that call for an Amen?

The Apostle Paul instructs us in Philippians 4:6 *"Do not be anxious about anything, but in everything, by prayer and petition, with thanksgiving, present your requests to God"* We read in Psalm 66:20 that God does not reject our prayer: *"Praise be to God, who has not rejected my prayer or withheld his love from me!"* He doesn't choose to listen to one person but not to another. He looks at the heart of the person, and when our prayer is sincere, that pleases Him.

In Luke 18:9–14 Jesus told the parable of the Pharisee and the tax collector. In Jesus' time the Pharisees were the teachers of the law. Many of them were very proud of their positions and thought they were better than other people. Jesus describes a Pharisee who went to the temple to pray. His prayer consisted of telling God how grateful he was not to be like other people. He made it clear that he was better than the tax collector who was at the temple at the same time. The Pharisee told God about his "righteous" behaviors for which he congratulated himself. In contrast, the tax collector asked God to have mercy on him, a sinner. Jesus said that only the tax collector went home justified before God *"For everyone who exalts himself will be humbled, and he who humbles himself will be exalted"* (Luke 18:14b).

When we pray, we must not puff ourselves up before Him. After all, we are talking about the omniscient One, God Almighty. He already knows all the good and bad things about us. We should approach Him with an understanding that it is only by His mercy and grace that we can speak directly to Him—not because we are good or because we have done some "good" deeds. It is only because of Jesus' shed blood on the cross that we are allowed into God's presence. Yes, He loves us and wants to have fellowship with us, and yes, we can approach Him with confidence (Hebrews 4:16), but not arrogance.

One last note: Some people may think that to pray, we are always supposed to be still, with folded hands and kneeling. There are times in our lives when we need to pray on our knees or even prostrate ourselves before Him. However, most of our daily prayer with our Lord occurs while we are working, doing the dishes, washing clothes, or even golfing. We are blessed to be able to have ongoing prayer conversations with our Lord because He is always with us.

Many years ago, I was shopping for a new devotional. All I could find were books with "a word for the day" format, and I was looking for something that would be filled with Scripture and a message. I told the Lord that I was extremely disappointed in the offerings of this very large Christian bookstore. He very clearly spoke to my mind, "Then write your own." From then on, He showed me how many happenings in our everyday lives relate to His Word and can have a special message. After a while, I had my first book, *Lord, It's Time for Just You and Me.* Since then, He very graciously blesses me with more ideas for consecutive books. I am humbled by what He has given me, and I am even more humbled that He loves me, listens to me, and takes time to teach me. In Jeremiah 33:3, God says, *"Call to me and I will answer you, and will tell you great and hidden things that you have not known"* (ESV). He does this for me, and He will do it for you. The Scripture doesn't say, "Cheryl Lynn Betz, call to me and I will answer you." No, that Scripture is for anyone who will take Him at His Word and call Him. Ask Him for what you need and listen for His still small voice.

Plan of Action

1. Spend some time thanking God for allowing you to pray to Him.
2. Now spend some time thinking of others you know who do not seem to know Jesus as Savior and Lord. Make note of them in a book and pray for their salvation. Put the date next to your prayer on their behalf. This is not like the prayer of the Pharisee. You pray for your friends because you have compassion on them, and you want them to have faith in Jesus alone for their salvation. Again, we know that it is only by His grace that we are saved. We have eternal life with

Him not because we did anything special and not because we are anyone special. Out of His love, He chose us and made a way for us to live with Him eternally. There is no room for arrogance here.

3. Often, prayer changes how we see others. If you know someone you don't like, and you see her often, or perhaps you think of her often, pray for her. Ask God to show you something admirable in her.

Prayer

My precious Lord and God, thank You for creating us with a desire to know You and to commune with You. Thank You for sending the Holy Spirit to live in us. How gracious You are to love us and to want to teach us. Please remind us to look to You for help and guidance. We love You, Lord, and we pray in Jesus' name. Amen.

> *"Praise be to God, who has not rejected my prayer or withheld his love from me"* (Psalm 66:20)!

Our God is so wonderful! He loves to answer our prayers.

COVET—YOU SHALL NOT

Scripture Reading: 1 Corinthians 12:4–31

"You shall not covet your neighbor's wife. You shall not set your desire on your neighbor's house or land, his male or female servant, his ox or donkey, or anything that belongs to your neighbor" (Deuteronomy 5:21).

We have lovely neighbors who invited us to their home for dinner. While there, I noticed that Jill had a wonderful, large refrigerator that had all kinds of room in it. I told her that I was trying hard not to covet her fridge. She and I laughed. At that time, we had a very small refrigerator, which the builder had included in the purchase price for our home. We guessed that our fridge was as large as the space could accommodate.

Not long after having dinner with our friends, I bought a new, blue purse with a braided shoulder strap, which Jill loved. She told me that she was trying hard not to covet my purse. I said, "Jill, you can afford to buy this purse." To which she replied, "And you can afford to buy our fridge." This was a joke of ours for a while.

A few months later, our refrigerator quit working, and we pulled it out of its space to take measurements. Guess what! The builder had put a spacer behind our fridge to make it set flush with our cabinets. We had room for the large refrigerator like our neighbors! Once we purchased a new, larger fridge and placed it in our kitchen, I took a photo of it and texted Jill. "Look what we have!" Then I explained the scenario that led to our having a new fridge. Jill's response was, "Does this mean I can't covet your purse anymore?" Of course, I replied, "Jill, you can afford to buy this purse." And we both had a good laugh. Jill and I knew we were kidding with each other.

Have you ever looked at another Christian and wished you had her confidence in speaking before a large group? Or perhaps you attend a Bible study, and you wish you were as skilled in teaching as others are. If you have been studying the Scripture for very long, you know that God gives gifts to all His children. That means you and me. He gives spiritual gifts to us so we can serve to build up His body—the church. He knows how He wants us to serve. We need to find out what our gifts are and then use them to His glory.

Furthermore, we need to be careful not to fall into the temptation of wanting another person's spiritual gifts or ministries. The Apostle Paul explained how important it is to embrace the gifts that God gives us and not desire the gifts that God has chosen to give others. First Corinthians 12:21 *"The eye cannot say to the hand, 'I don't need you!' And the head cannot say to the feet, 'I don't need you!"* In later verses, Paul emphasizes his point when he asks if God made us all apostles, prophets, teachers, so on. No, we need each person working in the church using his and her gifts.

Like you, I have been placed in many circles of relationships—my family, my church, my Bible study, my neighborhood, and my vocation—to exercise my gifts. In my case, I am an encourager and teacher. Mostly, I am to be salt and light to my fellow Christians. However, occasionally He uses me to show His light and spread His salt among people who don't yet know Him (Matthew 5:13–16).

If I try to be anyone other than the woman God made me, not only will I not be His best at it, but I will be squandering the gifts God has given me. I will also be standing in the way of the person who is supposed to minister to the group with that gift. This is probably most apparent with someone who cannot say no when asked to fill a position. She will become too busy trying to fill too many roles, and she will probably get burned out because of overextending herself. Another result of taking on too many roles could be that her reputation suffers because people find they can't depend on her.

God is very generous. He has created us to fill a spot in His world, and He knows what will fulfill us in the life He has given us. He knows where we are needed, and He arranged our location (Acts 17:26). He loves us, wants His best for us, and has gifted us to serve His body here on earth.

Plan of Action

1. If you don't know what your spiritual gifts are, please look for a reliable way to discover your gifts. I have found redletterchallenge.com to be a helpful resource for identifying my spiritual gifts. If you spend a few minutes taking the quiz at this website, it can help you start identifying what your gifts are. Be sure to answer the questions honestly. Don't answer how you wish you were. Answer honestly or taking the test will be a waste of time.

2. Once you know your gifts, look for opportunities to use them. You may already be doing this because we typically exercise our gifts even before we recognize them as gifts from God. The Apostle Paul admonished Timothy to *"fan into flame the gift of God"* which was in him by *"the laying on of my hands"* (2 Timothy 1:6). We are to use the gifts He has given us to His glory. Fan them into flame.

Prayer

Father, You love Your church, and You want it to work efficiently and effectively. You are generous to give us gifts of the Holy Spirit. Help us to walk in those gifts with a humble attitude, knowing that the gifts belong to You, and they are to bring glory to You, not to us. We are given these gifts to serve You and our church. Thank You, Lord. Please help us to never become prideful regarding our gifts or to covet the gifts of our fellow Christians. We pray in Jesus' name. Amen.

> *"Every good and perfect gift is from above, coming down from the Father of heavenly lights, who does not change like shifting shadows"* (James 1:17).

DROPPING PANSIES

Scripture Reading: Luke 17:11–19

"Jesus asked, 'Were not all ten cleansed? Where are the other nine?" (Luke 17:17).

When our daughter and I were leaving the hospital where my husband had just had open heart surgery, she made a point to say thank you to every person employed by the hospital. She meant every thank you, and I believe they knew and appreciated that. I immediately thought that her expressing her gratitude for how they were taking care of her father was as though she was dropping pansies, dropping beautiful flowers all along their paths to brighten up their day, to bless them. I am sure that was not the first time someone thanked them for doing their job. There cannot be too much sincere gratitude expressed in our lives.

Paul states in 1 Corinthians 10 verse 31, "*So whether you eat or drink, or whatever you do, do all to the glory of God*" (ESV). Therefore, no legitimate job is better than another. From my point of view, I am grateful that I can rely on others to fill certain roles such as being urologists, roofers, and trash collectors, to name a few.

As long as we do our jobs well, giving all glory to God, He is honored and blessed. In 1 Corinthians 12, Paul explains that there are different spiritual gifts and that all the gifts are given for the common good. Just as Christians are given different gifts for the common good, societies are made up of all kinds of occupations that work for our common good. We need farmers, scientists, doctors, teachers, trash collectors, authors, electricians, engineers, bus drivers, and so on. Each of these professions is important to our everyday lives. We should remember to express our gratitude when appropriate.

In the Scripture reading above, we have the story of the ten men who had leprosy. They asked Jesus to heal them, and when they were healed, only one of them returned to Jesus to thank Him and to give praise to God. I don't want to be like the nine who didn't bother to return to Jesus to give thanks.

Plan of Action

1. This might be a good time to make a call or write a note to someone for whom you are grateful. Drop a few pansies.

2. Let's decide today to live our lives giving thanks to those who serve us in one way or another and especially giving thanks to God for all He does for us.

Prayer

Lord, please quicken our thoughts to give thanks to people who serve us in some way. Father, we thank You for loving us. We thank You for sending Jesus so that our lives are made new living in Your kingdom. We thank Jesus for giving us abundant life. Help us to live lives of gratitude to You and to those You place in our paths. We pray in Jesus' name. Amen.

EGYPT AFTER THE EXODUS

Scripture Reading: Exodus 3:1–14; 5:1–5

"During the night Pharaoh summoned Moses and Aaron and said, 'Up! Leave my people, you and the Israelites! Go, worship the LORD as you have requested. Take your flocks and herds, as you have said, and go. And also bless me'" (Exodus 12:31–32).

I am sure that most of you remember the account in Exodus 1–12:30 when God directed Moses to tell Pharaoh to let the Israelites leave Egypt. Since *"the Israelites were fruitful and multiplied greatly and became exceedingly numerous"* (Exodus 1:7), Pharaoh feared them and put slave masters over them. They were a large part of Egypt's labor force, and therefore, he refused to let them go. Instead, he increased their workload and made their lives miserable. Then finally, after the ten plagues that the Lord set upon the Egyptians, Pharaoh told Moses and Aaron to leave Egypt and take all the Israelites with them (Exodus 12:31–32). The Lord told Moses to have the Israelites ask the Egyptians for silver and gold and clothing, and since He made the Egyptians *"favorably disposed"* toward the Israelites, *"they gave them what they asked for"* (Exodus 12:36).

Just imagine Egypt after the Israelites were gone. Since they were so numerous, they would have left quite a void, not only in a population plunge but also in the labor field. Suddenly, the Egyptians had to do the work the Israelites had done. Yet Psalm 105:37–38 says that the Egyptians were glad when the Israelites left. Exodus 12:37 states that there were *"about six hundred thousand men on foot, besides women and children."* Then we read in Exodus 14:5 that the king of Egypt is surprised that the Israelites had fled. Really?! He told them to leave. I suppose he may have thought they wouldn't go. After all, they had been in Egypt for four hundred thirty years (Exodus 12:40). Slavery in Egypt was all they had ever known. The Pharaoh's surprise doesn't seem so far out of the possible when we consider that sometimes people choose what's familiar instead of risking something new, even if the familiar is dreadful.

Did you note Pharaoh's request at the end of Exodus 12:32? Interesting that he wanted God's messengers, Moses and Aaron, with whom he had been arguing throughout the plagues, to bless him. That is hard to believe until we realize that with God's last plague on the Egyptians, every family was mourning the death of their firstborn son. Exodus 12:30 states that *"there was loud wailing in Egypt, for there was not a house without someone dead."* The Israelites were protected from this last plague because God had instructed them to put the blood of lambs on their doorframes so as He went throughout Egypt, He would pass over those homes (Exodus 12:3–13).

If you would like to read again about God's call on Moses, his leading the Israelites through their exodus from Egypt, and eventually entering the Promised Land, read Psalm 105:23–45.

Plan of Action

1. In the United States of America, slavery is against the law. When we need electrical work, we hire an electrician. When our sink is clogged to the point we can't correct it, we call a plumber. When our cars need work, we take them to repair shops. We hire people to do work for us when we don't know how to do it. The people whom we hire are not our slaves. We pay them for their expertise. We would be in quite a fix without them.

2. Just as *"the LORD made the Egyptians favorably disposed toward the people"* (Exodus 12:36), we know that even today He makes people favorably disposed toward His children—you and me. Therefore, when we receive an unexpected gift or compliment, let's remember that the praise goes to God, the giver of every good and perfect gift (James 1:17). If we have a sought-after skill that enhances others' lives, the Creator of the universe gave us that skill, and He gets the glory.

Prayer

Lord, thank You for always looking after us, protecting us, guiding us, loving us. Please open our eyes to see You at work in our lives. Give us grateful hearts and attitudes. Deliver us from unwarranted prejudice. Deliver us from greed and hate. I ask that by Your grace You form us into gentlemen and gentlewomen, full of Your love and Your kindness. Again, Lord, by Your gift of grace help us to forgive as You call us to. Please help us to bless You and to bless others in Your name. It is in the precious name of Jesus that we pray. Amen.

FEAR

Scripture Reading: Psalm 27

"And now O Israel, what does the Lord your God ask of you but to fear the Lord your God, to walk in all his ways, to love him, to serve the Lord your God with all your heart and with all your soul, and to observe the Lord's commands and decrees that I am giving you today for your own good" (Deuteronomy 10:12–13)?

"Fear not, for I am with you. Do not be dismayed. I am your God. I will strengthen you; I will help you; I will uphold you with my victorious right hand" (Isaiah 41:10 TLB).

Though it looks like the two Scriptures quoted above contradict each other, we know that they don't. In Deuteronomy 10:12, our Lord is telling us several things He wants of us, one of which is to fear Him. We also know this is a healthy fear. Fearing God means we take Him very seriously. God made us. God loves us. And God wants the best for us. We can trust Him to fulfill His many promises and to provide guidance in our lives. He wants us to fear Him more than anyone else. Again, this is a healthy fear.

Another healthy fear to have is the fear of danger. We teach our children not to touch a hot stove or oven. We teach our children to look for cars when crossing the street. We instruct them not to walk off with a stranger. If we are in danger, fear is easy and understandable. This is an excellent time to pull out some of those Scriptures we have memorized. It's amazing that when we speak His Word, we are calmed and encouraged at the same time. His Word is power. *"Though I walk in the midst of trouble, you preserve my life; you stretch your hand against the anger of my foes; with your right hand you save me"* (Psalm 138:7). Isn't that a great Scripture?

Many years ago, my husband was working late at the hospital. It was a lovely evening, and I had my kitchen window open. Suddenly, I heard someone walking in our backyard. It shook me because there was no reason for someone to be there. I calmly closed the window and checked to be sure the doors were locked. The Lord immediately reminded me of a Scripture I had memorized:

> *The LORD is my light and my salvation; whom shall I fear? When evil men come to destroy me, they will stumble and fall! Yes, though a might army marches against, my heart shall know no fear! I am confident that God will save me.*
> —Psalm 27:1–3 TLB

As I said this Scripture aloud, the fear left me. It was absolutely amazing! I was no longer afraid . . . at all!

Sometimes, God gives us the opportunity to share our faith with someone, but fear can keep us from following God's leading to share our faith with someone who needs to hear it. But when we realize God is directing us to speak to someone, we have to ask ourselves, "Do I fear God more than this person?" How will I feel if I lose the opportunity? We must decide whether we are more concerned with being embarrassed by sharing our faith with others than we are with disappointing God. When Jesus gave the marching orders for Christians in Matthew 28:18–20, He meant them for all of us:

> *All authority in heaven and on earth has been given to me. Therefore go and make disciples of all nations, baptizing them in the name of the Father and of the Son and of the Holy Spirit, and teaching them to obey everything I have commanded you. And surely I am with you always, to the very end of the age.*

When He tells us to do something, He will always help us to do it. Remember that He is with us all day every day.

I was taught many years ago that if I needed God to give me a direction as to where He wanted me to go but I didn't feel that I was hearing Him answer me, I needed to at least begin with a step forward. Sometimes, He leads us one step at a time. But we do need to take a step while trusting He'll direct us with each step. I love the story in Joshua 3 when God told Joshua what was required for the Israelites to cross the Jordan River on their way to the Promised Land. "*Now the Jordan is at flood stage. . . . Yet as soon as the priests . . . reached the Jordan and their feet touched the water's edge, the water from upstream stopped flowing. It piled in a heap a great distance away*" (Joshua 3:15–16). The priests in obedience to God's direction stepped into what would have been the Jordan at flood stage, and God held the water away from all the Israelites until they had crossed, all of them with dry feet. Don't you love that?! Nothing is impossible with God! But they had to take the step in faith. We too take the step in faith.

When we are afraid of going in the wrong direction, that fear can leave us going nowhere at all. If you find yourself in this dilemma, you might be encouraged by reviewing the resources in Appendix II in the back of this book. I have listed many Scriptures that record how the Lord leads us step by step. He doesn't always tell us our entire future or even our destination. He wants us to trust Him and move with Him in faith.

Our God created the heavens and the earth. Everything that exists was created by God. Therefore, we must place our hope and all we are in His care. He created us, He loves us, and He is more than able to protect us. Psalm 139:5 states, *"You both precede me and follow me, and place your hand of blessing on my head"* (TLB). We are never lost from Him.

Plan of Action

1. If you would like to read more Scriptures that speak of God's presence to erase fear, speak the words "Scriptures about fear" into your smart phone or use your internet search engine to find answers.

2. You might want to write down some of the Scriptures you find on index cards and carry them with you or put them where you will see them often, perhaps on your mirror or on your desk.

Prayer

Lord, throughout Your word, You tell us not to be afraid and at the same time, we are to fear You. You have given us life. You give us every breath. Our lives are literally in Your hands. Yet as we fear You, we know that You love us and will protect us. God, please take away all our unwarranted fears. As we have taught children to fear touching a hot stove or going into a busy street, we know there are certain things we should avoid. You give us wisdom and help. Please open our ears to hear You guiding us. Thank You, our loving Lord. We pray in Jesus' name. Amen.

FEIGNED INTEREST

Scripture Reading: John 13:34–35

"The LORD does not look at the things man looks at. Man looks at the outward appearance, but the LORD looks at the heart" (1 Samuel 16:7b).

I believe I have mentioned before that in some things I tend to be slow in catching on to certain people's behavior. Today in pool aerobics, there were sixteen women in our community pool who were trying to hear instructions over the noise of electric saws, hammers, and jackhammers. Our community was expanding our pool house.

When I saw that the ladies who were the farthest from the speaker couldn't hear the instructions, I shouted them out over the noise. How could they do the exercise if they couldn't hear? It wasn't until well into the hour that I figured out that they were only feigning interest in our program. They had purposely chosen the spots at the back of the group because they really didn't care if they heard the instructions. They wanted to have the appearance of exercising with us, but they were doing their own thing while visiting with each other. Once I realized that, I stopped shouting over the construction noise.

This is not unlike people who attend church with feigned interest. They want everyone around them to think they are Christians worshipping God and growing in their faith. The reasons for these masquerades are probably as varied as the people who act them out. Perhaps it is to look good for their business or to appease a parent or a spouse.

Churches can make all kinds of changes to their worship services to attract these people with the hope of converting them. But until these people are enlightened by the Holy Spirit, they will continue with their masquerade no matter what alterations churches make.

It is the privilege and responsibility of all Christians to answer to God for our behavior, whether we are in the sanctuary for worship, in Sunday School, at work, or at home. He has called us to love others: Christians and masqueraders. Since we may not be able to distinguish between the two, we love without prejudice. *"God's love has been poured into our hearts through the Holy Spirit who has been given to us"* (Romans 5:5b).

For those who are called to lead whether in the worship service or Sunday school or wherever, we need to remember that we cannot always tell by the looks on people's faces whether they are listening or not. We must deliver what the Lord has given us and leave the rest of the work to Him.

We should also take this as encouragement for those of us who have friends with whom we have shared Christ but see no acceptance or change. The conversion is the Lord's work. God sees their hearts. We live as we are supposed to as Christians and leave the changing to Him.

Plan of Action

1. Take a few minutes to list friends who have not accepted Jesus as their Savior. If you don't have a journal to keep track of your prayer requests, I suggest you get one. List your requests next to their names and dates of your prayers.

2. If you have not written a note of encouragement to your pastor lately, now would be a good time to do that. It only takes a moment, and it will be a blessing to them.

Prayer

Lord, our churches have the responsibility to preach and teach Your Word accurately and without apology. Please help them to do that. Please protect the pastors and other leaders and their families from the enemy's arrows. Thank You for their answering Your call on their lives. Please bless them, Lord. Help us to love them well. Thank You for teaching us to love. In Jesus' name. Amen.

A GOD APPOINTMENT

Scripture Reading: Acts 8:26–40

"From one man he made every nation of men, that they should inhabit the whole earth; and he determined the times set for them and the exact places where they should live" (Acts 17:26).

In our 1500-member church in Florida, my husband and I greeted Jane who used to live in Ohio where she and her family attended the same church as our daughter. Her daughter and ours are very good friends. Since Jane's daughter was visiting from Ohio, she wanted me to meet her. After wading through several people, we finally reached her daughter. As I shook her hand, she informed me that she had just texted our daughter to say that she hoped she would be able to meet her mom (me). What a circle of interesting connections! Wow.

Could you follow the sequence of events? My point is that God knows what is important to His children, and He arranges the necessary connections for us. How kind of Him! He truly loves us and loves to bless us. Proverbs 8:17 states, *"I love those who love me, and those who seek me find me."* First John 3:1a reminds us *"How great is the love the Father has lavished on us, that we should be called children of God! And that is what we are!"*

Intriguingly, there are several interesting connections the Lord has arranged for us in our church. To become members of our church, we went to a six-week course, which explained what our responsibilities as members would be and how our church operated. During this course, we became fond of a young woman who came to the class wearing a Kansas City Chief's jersey. We explained that we, too, were Chief's football fans although we had moved away from Kansas City many years ago. She introduced us to her mother, and in the process of our discussion, we found out that her mother was a high school cheerleader with my sister in Kansas!

A few weeks later, again in our large church in Florida, we recognized a couple who still attend our church in Kansas City. In fact, when we lived in Kansas City, we served together on the same Youth Board. One of the pastors in our Florida church grew up in Lawrence, Kansas, which is just outside Kansas City, and he went to Kansas University. On our river cruise in France, we met and became friends with two couples from the Kansas City Area. It was fun catching up on how the city has changed.

Because the Lord so often connects us with someone from our past, both at home in Florida and when we travel, my husband is truly surprised when we don't meet someone we know. In fact, when our kids were still living with us and we would take a trip, my husband and our daughter would have a bit of competition as to who would be the first to meet someone they knew.

I believe the Lord arranges these surprise connections to confirm that we are where we are supposed to be and because He wants to bless us and others. As we travel, we are His ambassadors just as we are His ambassadors at home (2 Corinthians 5:20). We have the responsibility of behaving in a way that will draw others to us and, therefore, through us to Him. It doesn't mean that we preach to everyone we meet. It does mean that we allow the fruit of the Holy Spirit to flow through us and to touch others. As a close friend and I were wrapping up a day of shopping, she said, "Cheryl Lynn, you are so kind to everyone we meet." I am not writing this to make you think I am perfect by any means. Honestly, I had never considered that I was unusually kind to others that we had encountered, and I was surprised that my behavior was noteworthy to her. I give all praise to God who is at work changing me to be more like His Son (Romans 8:29). There are still lots of personality traits and behaviors that the Lord is working out of me. Just remember that our God is a gentleman, and we should be gentlemen and gentlewomen.

For those of you who are parents, think of a time when you gave your child something wonderful as a surprise. Do you remember how pleased, maybe even excited the child was? God is our Father, and as I said before, He loves us and loves to bless us.

Plan of Action

1. Take a few moments to think of the many blessings the Lord has given you. I remember a saying that was common a while ago. What if you woke up tomorrow, and you only had what you had thanked God for the previous day? I don't want you to feel that you must go through the same extensive prayer list every day, but I do want you to realize how blessed you are because God loves you.

2. Ask the Lord to enlighten you of His divine appointments in your life. There are no coincidences in a Christian's life, only God appointments. Remind yourself that all day every day, we are His Ambassadors.

Prayer

Father, please give me eyes to see, ears to hear, and a heart to obey You. In the Scripture Reading at the beginning of today's devotion, we read how You told Phillip to go the chariot and stay near it. He obeyed and was there at the exact time that the man was reading Isaiah53:7–8, which he did not understand. But Lord, You put Phillip there to explain it to him and to bring that man into Your Kingdom. As we go through our days, please don't let us miss Your appointments. Help us to be sensitive to Your moves and to follow Your lead all to Your glory. Thank You, Lord. We pray in the precious and powerful name of Jesus. Amen.

GOD HEALED ME

Scripture Reading: Isaiah 53:1–12

"He himself bore our sins in his body on the tree, that we might die to sin and live to righteousness. By his wounds you have been healed" (1 Peter 2:24).

When I was eight years old, I began having migraine headaches. First, I would have blank spots in my vision. That was my warning that the migraine was coming very soon. If I was at school when it hit, I had to go to the office and call my dad to come get me. Then I would go home, lie on the couch, block out all light, and pray there would be no noise. The migraines would last several hours, and they were horrible. I had migraines several times a year until I was twenty-five.

I was driving home from work listening to Christian radio when a preacher with a very gravelly voice came on. I reached to change the station, and God said very clearly in my mind, "Don't change the station. Ignore the gravelly sound of his voice. Listen to the message." The pastor was telling me that Christ had died in my place and by His wounds I have been healed. I had no doubt that this was His message for me. He wanted to heal me of the migraines. Therefore, I spoke out loud, "Yes, Lord. By Your wounds, I am healed. Thank You, Lord." I had no doubt that there and then Christ healed me of migraine headaches. From that day to this as I am writing in 2024, I have not had a migraine headache. I have had very minor headaches but nothing like a migraine.

Why did that work for me that day? I don't know. But I praise God that He told me to continue listening to the preacher, and I praise Him for healing me. I wonder why He doesn't heal others from those horrible, debilitating migraines. I know several people who have them, and I ask, even to this day, for God to heal them as He did me. I understand that there is medication now to help prevent them from coming. Praise God for that! I am a firm believer in His performing miracles through medicine.

I am telling you this just in case you have a chronic illness. Remain open to the possibility of Christ healing you. Listen to what He says to you and obey. In 2 Kings 5:1–16, Naaman had leprosy, and his wife's servant told her that if he could see the prophet Elisha in Samaria, he would heal him. When Naaman went to the door of Elisha, the prophet sent a messenger to him instructing him to wash himself seven times in the Jordan and he would be healed. However, Naaman was angry because he expected Elisha to come to him and do something physical so he could be healed. So he ignored Elisha's words. But when Naaman's servants saw that he had ignored Elisha's directions, they reasoned with him enough that Naaman did what Elisha had instructed and was healed. If you haven't read this Bible story, you should. It's not long.

Then there is the thirty-eight-year-old invalid in John 5. Jesus asked him, "*Do you want to get well?*" The man answered that he had tried to get into the pool to get healing. But others always entered the pool before him, and therefore he was still an invalid. Jesus said to him, "*Get up! Pick up your mat and walk.*" The man was cured.

What I want you to see is that God heals each person in His own way. There are many recordings in the Bible about Jesus healing people, and they are all different. He made us all unique, and He ministers to us according to our needs. It is only logical that He would pattern our cure in His own way. If you need to be healed, God knows. He loves you, and He wants the best for you. Someone told me once that God always answers our prayers with yes, no, or not yet. Look to Him for what you need, and trust Him to take care of you.

Plan of Action

1. If you are praying for God to heal you, don't lose heart. He wants only the best for you, and His plan for you is wonderful. Open your ears and eyes and have an open heart to Him. Read the story in Luke 18:1–8 in which a woman continued to approach a judge who didn't want to deal with her. But she didn't give up. The judge finally gave in to her because she so persistently confronted him, and he was tired of her. That story is told to encourage us to keep praying and not to give up.

2. If you know someone who wants to receive healing, please pray for them right now. Prayer is powerful, and God has told us to pray for ourselves and others.

Prayer

Father, I praise You again for healing me from migraine headaches. I ask that, just as You healed me as I listened to the radio preacher, You heal everyone reading this who needs a cure. I know that sometimes You heal supernaturally, and sometimes You heal through medicine. For those whose answer from You is "not yet," I pray that You encourage them as they live with their illness or disability. I know that You love us. Let each person reading this know that You love him or her. In Jesus' precious and powerful name. Amen.

"LORD my God, I called to you for help,
and you healed me" (Psalm 30:2).

Thank You, Lord.

GOD HEALED MY HUSBAND

Scripture Reading: Acts 9:32–43

"O LORD my God, I cried to you for help, and you healed me" (Psalm 30:2).

"Bless the LORD, O my soul, and forget not all his benefits, who forgives all your iniquity, who heals all your diseases" (Psalm 103:2–3 ESV).

In 1995, my husband, a physician, had a new x-ray machine and decided to test it. He had his technician X-ray his chest. The result showed a five-centimeter mass in the center of his chest, next to his heart and lungs. The next day a doctor took a biopsy, and it was determined that he had small-cell inoperable lung cancer. When I arrived home, I called everyone I knew who believed in prayer. I cried through telling them the diagnosis and asked them to pray.

At that time, a small-cell lung cancer patient was looking at a 30 percent, five-year survival rate, but they were usually dead within two years. He underwent one week of chemotherapy with three weeks off, which did nothing to the tumor but was brutally hard on him. It aged him ten years. His oncologist, who was one of my husband's friends, decided to send him to Memorial Sloan Kettering in New York.

We met with a surgeon who looked at Bill's recent medical history and said, "Well, I don't know what it is, but it can't be small-cell cancer. It would be best in the bucket." And then she pointed to the waste basket. In other words, she believed it would be best to surgically remove it. Suddenly, that which was inoperable was now operable. We saw her on Friday, and his surgery was on Monday. The mass was well-circumscribed, and they were able to surgically remove all of it. It was called a surgical cure.

Interestingly, the tumor was a primitive neuroectodermal tumor of the mediastinum, referred to as a PNET. This type of tumor had only been seen in teenage boys. My husband was in his forties. Praise God it had not invaded his lungs or heart, and he has been cancer-free for all these years.

One night, during one of his weeks off from chemotherapy, I was alone in our bedroom and trying to pray. I just kept repeating, "Lord, the statistics for survival of lung cancer are so bad." Suddenly, the Lord stopped me and spoke very distinctly and firmly in my mind. "Don't worry about statistics! I make them!" What a weight He lifted off my shoulders. I had such peace. I ran to the other room where Bill was and said, "The Lord just told me that we don't have to worry about the statistics because He makes them!" I was so excited that I repeated what He said to us many times through this battle.

One of the reasons I am writing about this is to show that God can change the diagnosis. He can change the inoperable to operable. Another reason I am writing this is to impress upon you how important it is for people to pray for those who are ill or going through a tough time. Like us, those people many times find it hard to pray because they are so consumed with what is going on in their lives. While we were going through this, my mind was racing so much of the time, I could hardly pray. We are immeasurably grateful for all the people from all over the United States who were praying for us.

Plan of Action

1. If you are in a battle for your health, ask others to pray for you. No matter what the illness, God is not surprised by this. Lean on Him as He is always strong and capable of comforting His loved ones. I don't know why God heals some people and not others. I have heard that God looks at those He chooses not to heal as strong and able to handle the illness or disability. I really don't know. But I do know He loves His creation, and each one of us is His creation.

2. If you know someone who is going through a battle whether it is physical or mental, pray for them. Consider sending them a card of encouragement. There are some very good cards out there. But again, please pray for them because they need your prayers.

Prayer

Father, I am grateful that You know what we are going through, and You are in charge of our lives. I know many people who are fighting serious illnesses, and I ask You, Lord, please heal them. For those who are reading this, Lord, I ask that You heal them too. Please encourage them and put Your loving arms around them. You are all powerful, and nothing is impossible for You. We love You, Lord. Please extend Your healing power to those reading this and to the people I know who are so discouraged. Thank You for loving us. Remind us to extend the love You give us to others. In Jesus' name. Amen.

> "LORD my God, I called to you for help,
> and you healed me" (Psalm 30:2).

Thank You, Lord.

GOD IS NOT DONE WITH YOU

Scripture Reading: Philippians 1:18–26

"Teach us to number our days that we may get a heart of wisdom" (Psalm 90:12).

"For I know the plans I have for you" declares the Lord, *"plans to prosper you and not to harm you, plans to give you hope and a future"* (Jeremiah 29:11).

The Apostle Paul was in prison in chains when he wrote the letter to the Philippians (Philippians 1:17b). He felt divided because he knew when he died, he would be with Christ, but he also knew he needed to continue to stay on earth and help others progress in their faith and joy (Philippians 1:25). According to Scripture, as long as we are alive in this universe, God is not done with us. He always has purpose for our lives. *"For we are God's workmanship, created in Christ Jesus to do good works, which God prepared in advance for us to do"* (Ephesians 2:10).

The Westminster Catechism asks this question, "What is the chief end of man?" Our answer is: To glorify God and enjoy Him forever. We are all supposed to glorify God in whatever we do and to enjoy Him forever. Let's make this personal. Do you know what God wants to do through you? What good works are you supposed to do? Do you know why you are here? This is the question the Lord asked me decades ago when He pulled me back into life in Him. He allowed me to get to a place in my life where I desperately needed to know there was a purpose for my life. I was depressed and lonely for many reasons including the fact that my husband was gone for two weeks of training for his new job. I had drifted away from the church and Christian fellowship and had lost track of my spiritual life in Christ. Add to that sorry state of being, I was bored, and I hate to be bored!

I was so bored that I decided to read a couple of books that my mother had given me. Of course, she had no idea how far I had drifted from the Lord nor how the Lord would use those books to change my life. One of the books was *Beyond Ourselves*, by Catherine Marshall, followed by another of her books called *Something More*. Through her writing, God reminded me that Jesus was my dearly loved Savior. He shed His blood on my behalf, which cleansed away my sin. In addition, He saved me from depression by speaking through Catherine Marshall's work, which pointed out that He did indeed love me and had a purpose and a plan for my life. I thank God for Catherine Marshall and her many books. As God's plans are always perfect, even now decades later, He continues to hold me fast and use me everywhere He takes me as I love, teach, and lead His beloved as He loves, teaches, and leads me. What a generous Lord!

After reading Catherine Marshall's books, I read several of Norman Vincent Peale's books. I was a big-time worrier. Through Mr. Peale's writings, the Lord taught me not to worry—well ... to worry less and pray more. Since Mr. Peale recommended memorizing Scripture, I started a notebook where I wrote down my favorite Scriptures and started to memorize them. This is also when I started a prayer notebook. I dated and listed my prayers, and when I saw Him answer them, I recorded the date next to the prayer.

The next books I read were *The Hiding Place* by Corrie ten Boom with John and Elizabeth Sherrill, and *God's Smuggler* by Brother Andrew with John and Elizabeth Sherrill, through which He revealed that even today He continues to work miracles. My appetite for all things Christian carried me through many other books by Christian authors who helped me grow further in my faith. Eventually, I returned to church and participated in Bible studies, prayer meetings, and other types of Christian fellowship.

When we get to heaven, I wonder if we will get to thank all those through whose work the Lord used to increase our faith. Can you imagine that, in addition to meeting Jesus and falling at His feet in pure adoration, we'll meet David, Ruth, Daniel, Peter, Paul, Stephen, and many more? I plan to hug my mother and father and thank them for guiding me back to Him. In due course, I will thank Catherine Marshall, Norman Vincent Peale, Brother Andrew, Corrie ten Boom, John and Elizabeth Sherrill, and the many other authors who contributed to building my faith in Christ.

The first Bible that I read when I realized that the Scripture was God's words for me was Kenneth Taylor's *The Living Bible*. I praise God for him. Although I was in my twenties at that time, I was still a babe when it came to reading Scripture, and *The Living Bible* was perfect for me. I still use it in my writing and teaching when I believe that Ken Taylor's paraphrase makes the Bible's verse clearer than other versions of the Bible.

The reason I am telling you all of this is to encourage you. I know He still has plans for both you and me. He continues to use us because the Holy Spirit is living in us, guiding us, working through us. As long as we have breath, He has a purpose for our lives. If you don't know what His plan is for you, ask Him and then listen for His answer. If you are not a member of a church, find one that preaches and teaches the Bible as God's living Word given to His people and understood because of the Holy Spirit. Christ is supreme and is regarded as such in a worthy church. If you are homebound, live-stream a worship service and teaching. When we travel, we live-stream our church's worship service by going to YouTube, and then we ask for Covenant Church, Naples, Florida. There we have many different Sunday services to select from. We usually choose the one going on that day. Sometimes, we go to YouTube and search for "Truth for Life" with Alistair Begg. He is a wonderful, Bible-preaching pastor. In addition to attending worship services, get involved in a local Bible study. We have several in our church as most churches do. We even have a very good one Bible study in our neighborhood. Look around. One of my very dear friends had a brother with ALS who led a Bible study in his nursing home. Now that you are aware and looking, you will find one.

Next, ask God what He wants you to do and be open to new opportunities that He will place in your path. It doesn't matter how old you are; He has a plan for you. I remember something my good friend Pam G likes to remind us: "If it is not right, it's not over." In other words, she is pointing us to Romans 8:28, which says, *"And we know that in all things God works for the good of those who love him, who have been called according to his purpose."* Granted we may not know the good He is working until we get to heaven. The promise is still there. Now look at Romans 8:28 again. Ask yourself, "Do I love God, and am I called for His purpose?" The answer to those questions is undoubtedly yes since you are reading this devotional. People who hate God and don't want to do what He wants are probably not going to read a Christian devotional. As a person who loves God and desires to be used for His purpose, He will work all things for your good.

Remember: God is not done with you until He calls you home, and even then, I believe that you and I will still have wonderful, enjoyable work to do for and with our beloved God the Father, God the Son, and God the Holy Spirit. Praise His holy name!

Plan of Action

1. Most of the time, God uses our training and education as He works His plans for our lives. However, sometimes, He gifts us anew while we are following His lead. If you don't think that you know why God put you where you find yourself, ask Him to make His plan known to you. Begin to look at your friends and your activities. That should give you a hint.

2. You can also seek help from your church. You might start volunteering for some activities where they need help. Both small and large churches need helpful people for lots of things. Through participating in different activities, you'll probably discover what He has, and even what He has not, called you to do.

Prayer

Lord, thank You so much for loving me. I am grateful for all You do. Please continue to lead me to do Your will. Make me a worthy vessel through whom You can love and bless others forever. In Jesus' name. Amen.

GOD, OUR CREATOR

Scripture Reading: Isaiah 45:18–25

"The earth is the Lord's, and everything in it, the world, and all who live in it; for he founded it upon the seas and established it upon the waters" (Psalm 24:1–2).

"Lord Almighty, God of Israel, enthroned between the cherubim, you alone are God over all the kingdoms of the earth. You have made heaven and earth" (Isaiah 37:16).

"Sovereign Lord . . . you made the heaven and the earth and everything in them" (Acts 4:24).

Looking through the airplane window on a recent trip, I decided that the mountain ranges with the rivers cutting through them resembled branches of plants; some of the plants had long dark green and yellow leaves, while others had shorter leaves. It was amazing how easy it was to see the comparison of the life carried by the rivers versus the life carried by the plant stems. It's funny that I had never seen the similarity before that day although I had flown hundreds of times.

The pattern of the farmers plowing or harvesting displayed as ribboned upholstery one might see in a sofa—in earth tones, of course. So many shapes. So many colors. I looked down on so many houses and buildings and cars filled with so many people. Yet God knows the count of every hair on every head (Luke 12:6–7). He even looks after the sparrows, and we're more important to Him than they are. How can He take care of all of us? We know He does because He says so in Matthew 6:25–34.

There is not a shape that wasn't created by God. There is not a color that wasn't created by God, not a mountain, not a field, not a texture, not a taste, not a person.

> *For by him all things were created: things in heaven and on earth, visible and invisible, whether thrones or powers or rulers or authorities; all things were created by him and for him. He is before all things, and in him all things hold together.*
>
> —Colossians 1:16–17

Miracle of miracles is Him abiding in me and me abiding in Him (John 15:4–9). The Creator of all abides in me. He abides in you too if you have accepted Christ as your Savior. Miracle of miracles!

Plan of Action

1. You might want to take some time to express your gratitude to God for the supreme way He takes care of you.

2. If you do not yet know Christ, this would be a good time for you to ask Him to make Himself real to you. He loves to reveal Himself when a person is sincerely seeking Him. He tells us that in the Bible, His Word. *"Ask and it will be given to you; seek*

and you will find; knock and the door will be opened to you. For everyone who asks receives; he who seeks finds; and to him who knocks, the door will be opened" (Matthew 7:7–8).

Prayer

Lord, You know that my mind cannot fully grasp how You can possibly take care of the entire universe. You placed the stars in the sky. You gave me life, and now You abide in me. Wow! Please let me honor You in everything I do and say. If I have a maverick thought or behavior, remind me that I am Yours and that I am Your representative to the world, those who know You and those who don't. I love You so much. All I am and all I have are Yours. Thank You, precious, loving, Lord. I pray in Jesus' name. Amen.

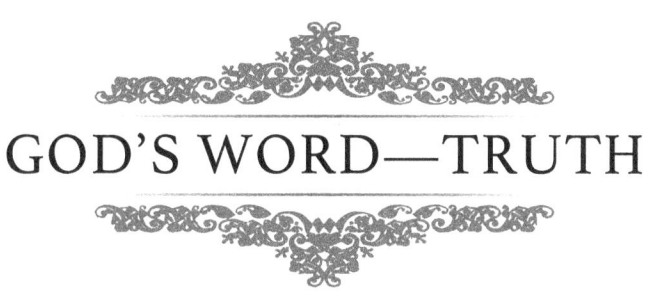

GOD'S WORD—TRUTH

Scripture Reading: 2 Timothy 3:14–17

"The earth is the LORD'S, and everything in it, the world, and all who live in it; for he founded it upon the seas and established it upon the waters" (Psalm 24:1–2).

"My son, give attention to my words; incline your ear to my sayings. . . . They are life to those who find them, and health to all their flesh (Proverbs 4:20, 22 NKJV).

"O LORD Almighty, God of Israel, enthroned between the cherubim, you alone are God over all the kingdoms of the earth. You have made heaven and earth" (Isaiah 37:16).

Many years ago, when I was just getting familiar with the Bible, my Scripture reading for the day was in Nehemiah. I wasn't sure where Nehemiah was in the Bible and, unlike some of my friends, I hadn't memorized the order of the books of the Bible. I thought Nehemiah was in front of the Psalms, so I thumbed through many books until I found it.

Of course, now, if I don't know where a book is, I go to the front of the Bible where the names and order of the books are listed with page numbers. But I didn't think of that then.

It occurred to me that had I searched after Psalms, I wouldn't have found it. I could have been diligent, going past every book, only to be disappointed. The point is that many people are systematically searching for the Truth, carefully, spending lots of time and maybe even money. But if they are looking in the wrong place, they won't find it.

This should tell us two things. First, sometimes people need help finding the Truth. Second, since we know where the Truth is, we need to be ready to help others to find it. It may be as simple as inviting a neighbor to church and being willing to answer questions that might arise:

> *Therefore go and make disciples of all nations, baptizing them in the name of the Father and of the Son and of the Holy Spirit, and teaching them to obey everything I have commanded you. And surely I am with you always, to the very end of the age.*
> —Matthew 28:19–20

That is Jesus' commission to us as believers. Whenever He asks something of us, He is already laying the groundwork for us to achieve it. Just follow His lead.

The Word of God generates life. God spoke and there was life (Genesis 1:20–28). He continues to bless us with not only living plants that we can eat but also those that give us shade and others that are beautiful for us to gaze upon. He blesses us with children to enjoy as well as to carry on our work and our faith (Psalm 127:3–5). Again, He has only to speak and there is life.

Because we know this, let's begin to speak His Word where we see death and even the threat of death.

Plan of Action

1. Take an objective view of your church. How do they treat God's Word? Are they preaching it? Are you getting fed, and are you growing spiritually?

2. If you answered no to the first question, find a new church. Although you are getting fed spiritually by reading this book and all the Scriptures that are listed, you need a good Bible-teaching church.

3. If you answered yes to the first question, look around. Is there someone you need to invite to your church?

Prayer

Thank You, Lord, for giving us ready access to Bibles. Most of us are blessed to have several Bibles in our homes. Thank You for being our Father and for Your love. Please help us to see where there are people who need You and need Your Word. Please give us discernment to see the difference between "a feel good" church and one that is led by Your Holy Spirit working through the leaders and a congregation that is ready and able to lead people to You. You amaze us. In Jesus' name. Amen.

HIS MANY BLESSINGS

Scripture Reading: Luke 17:11–19

"The Lord himself goes before you and will be with you; he will never leave you nor forsake you. Do not be afraid; do not be discouraged" (Deuteronomy 31:8).

If you have read many of my devotionals, you are aware that the Lord had us move from one city to another several times. On one move, He gave us Jeremiah 29:7: *"Also, seek the peace and prosperity of the city to which I have carried you into exile. Pray to the Lord for it, because if it prospers, you too will prosper."* Isn't that an awesome Scripture to receive right before He moved us to a new city? We loved that He gave us this specific message, and we even chuckled because He was moving us from a large city where we had lived all our lives to a remote city in the Appalachian Mountains.

Although it took us a bit of time to get used to the Kentucky accent, we loved living there. We loved the people there. We were helping to start a medical school, and the people accepted us with love. Before our graduates started their practices in the town, the people had to wait for months to see a doctor. After our graduates finished their residencies, many of them chose to begin their medical practices there in their hometown. What a blessing that was! Not only were the people able to get into a doctor much more quickly than before, but they also knew the men and women physicians who had grown up there. God allowed us to see some of the fruit of our labor.

The small town's population grew and flourished because of the influx of professors teaching at the medical school. Since most of the professors and students came from elsewhere, they had to find a place to live. These new residents were buying groceries, furniture, and frequenting the local restaurants. We, like others who moved there to help with the medical school, needed to find a doctor, a dentist, a hairdresser, a barber, a place where our cars could be serviced, a church, and so on. Suddenly, there were new people buying postage stamps, school supplies, greeting cards and getting pedicures and manicures. It was wonderful to see the town prosper.

I have mentioned in one of my other books what a short-term missionary told me years ago when we were in Ecuador: "Cheryl, God rarely does a one-way blessing. Most of the time, the person offering the blessing also receives a blessing." I am sure you have seen this in your own life. Christmas morning as you watch your family opening the gifts you have chosen for them, you are blessed by their pleasure. When you have served the homeless in a soup kitchen or taken a meal to a bereaving family, you are blessed not only by their reactions but also by knowing you are pleasing God. Perhaps someone has asked you to pray with them concerning a need or a problem. The Lord certainly blessed you both as you came to Him for help and direction. Our amazing, wonderful, incredible, loving God loves to bless us. He is our Father who is perfect and knows what we need before we ask (Matthew 6:8).

Let's remember to thank our Father for His many blessings. We should have the habit of considering where our blessings are from. In Luke 17:11–19, we read the account of Jesus healing ten men of leprosy, but only one returned to thank Him. Let's be the ones who always thank our Lord for His many blessings.

Plan of Action

1. Make it a habit of thanking God every time something good happens to you. You can either thank Him aloud or silently acknowledge that you know He arranged that for you. *"Every good and perfect gift is from above, coming down from the Father of the heavenly lights, who does not change like shifting shadows"* (James 1:17).

2. Keep in mind that ministering, helping, attending to the needs of others rarely finds us at a convenient time. However, if the Lord has presented the need before us, it is likely that our schedule can be altered to touch the one who is hurting, confused, or whatever. These people are not nuisances that interrupt our schedule; they are divine opportunities for us to serve as God's messengers.

Prayer

Lord, thank You for allowing us the opportunity to minister to those who are hurting and to those who are confused, or even just lonely. Move us to show them Your love. Help us to discern the real problem or issue so that together with You, we can bless them in their need. I am so in awe of You, Lord. When I think of how much You love us, I weep with gratitude. Lord, please help us to be a blessing to You in all that we do, by Your grace and in Jesus' name. Amen.

"May the favor of the Lord our God rest upon us; establish the work of our hands for us—yes, establish the work of our hands" (Psalm 90:17).

I AM A SINNER, FORGIVEN

Scripture Reading: Romans 5:1–8

"Then the LORD turned from his burning anger"
(Joshua 7:26b ESV).

Sometimes we think God is finished with us since we can't seem to get past our sin. Therefore, we ask ourselves how can God use us? The miraculous thing is that the Lord can and does continue to use us, and He continues to forgive our sins. He's not overlooking our sin, but He wants us to ask Him for forgiveness so we can move on with our lives! When we confess it, He erases it from our life record.

In Matthew 18:21 the Apostle Peter asked Jesus *how many times should he forgive his brother. "Up to seven times?" Jesus answered, 'I tell you, not seven times, but seventy-seven times'"* (Matthew 18:21b–22). Jesus was not saying that we literally forgive a person seventy-seven times. Instead, He is saying that there is not a limited number of times we are to forgive someone. Think of the many times God forgives us. He doesn't forgive seventy-seven times, and then that's it! No. God is constantly wooing us, showing us His love, forgiving us while He continues to teach us the way He wants us to live, forming us to be more like Christ. Praise His name!

Our God changes us while we read His Word (2 Timothy 3:16–17 and when we allow the Holy Spirit to work in our lives (John 14:15–17). He will faithfully help us to get past our sin and work with Him until that sin is no longer in our life. *"Do not conform any longer to the pattern of this world, but be transformed by the renewing of your mind. Then you will be able to test and approve what God's will is—his good, pleasing and perfect will"* (Romans 12:2). How do we renew our mind and know what God's will is? By reading God's Word and letting the Holy Spirit work His Word into our lives.

Second Corinthians 5:17 states: *"Therefore, if anyone is in Christ, he is a new creation; the old has passed away; behold, the new has come"* (ESV). As believers and followers of Christ, we are in Christ. When sin tempts us in our new creation, we call on Jesus to take away the temptation. He has promised us that He will work with us faithfully, tirelessly. We can rely on Him to help us when we are tempted. First Corinthians 10:13 states: *"No temptation has seized you except what is common to man. And God is faithful; he will not let you be tempted beyond what you can bear. But when you are tempted, he will also provide a way out so that you can stand up under it."* I particularly like the way Kenneth Taylor paraphrased the same Scripture in the *Living Bible*:

> *But remember this—the wrong desires that come into your life aren't anything new and different. Many others have faced exactly the same problems before you. And no temptation is irresistible. You can trust God to keep the temptation from becoming so strong that you can't stand up against it, for he has promised this and will do what he says. He will show you how to escape temptation's power so that you can bear up patiently against it.*

Once God forgives us, will we ever sin again? Sadly, we will. When we do, we should immediately confess it to our Lord and ask His forgiveness. Satan wants us to wallow in our sin state and say to ourselves that we will never get rid of this sin pattern. Don't wallow! Ask God's forgiveness. Accept His forgiveness and love. He can and will help you now and in the future. Satan wants to cripple you in your wallowing state. Don't let him! Jesus loves you so much that He took all sin upon Himself at the cross—yours, mine, and everyone else's. He did this so God could have fellowship with us because He loves us even in our sinful state. But He loves us enough not to leave us in sin.

"But God demonstrates his own love for us in this: While we were still sinners, Christ died for us" (Romans 5:8). Did you see the word *demonstrates?* That is written in the present tense as in right now. Today, He demonstrates His love for us. He knows we can't make ourselves good by ourselves. We must have the Holy Spirit working in us, changing us. Nevertheless, God loved us before we accepted Christ as our Savior. Christ died for us when we were sinners. How remarkable is that?! He loves us now and forever, and He will never leave or forsake us (Hebrews 13:5).

Be encouraged, sweet friends. Our Lord loves us and will continue to work with you and me until we see Christ face to face (1 Corinthians 13:12 and Revelation 22:3–4). Glory! Halleluiah!

Plan of Action

1. Psalm 139:23–24 in the *Revised Standard Version* says, *"Search me, O God, and know my heart! Try me and know my thoughts! And see if there be any wicked way in me, and lead me in the way everlasting!"* Ask the Lord to point out any sin that you have not yet confessed to Him. Then immediately ask Him for forgiveness. This might be a good way to start each day or to end each night.

2. As you look around and you see other sinners, pray for them. Don't dismiss anyone as unreachable. No one is out of God's reach. Remember the story in Mark 5:1–20 where a man was filled with demons who tormented him day and night. He wandered in the hills and tombs. The poor man had no peace until he met Jesus. Jesus cast the demons out of the man. This man's life became totally new! Not surprisingly he asked to go with Jesus, but Jesus told him: "*Go home to your friends, and tell them how much the Lord has done for you, and how he has had mercy on you*" (Mark 5:19 RSV). I don't know how many testimonies you have heard, but I know this one would make me sit up and pay attention to the miracles that God does. Again, no one is out of God's reach.

Prayer

Lord, You are truly amazing! Please keep me from writing people off as lost souls. You saved me when I was still a sinner. You saved the person reading this when he or she was a sinner. Thank You for forgiving us! Thank You for Your generosity! Thank You for Your wondrous power, which You graciously have given us by the Holy Spirit. Thank You for Your mercy and grace. Please help us to view others through Your eyes. We love You, Lord, and we pray in Jesus' name. Amen

AN INFLUENCER

Scripture Reading: Revelation 20:11–15

*"'For I know the plans I have for you'
declares the L*ORD*, "plans to prosper you and
not to harm you, plans to give you hope and a future"'
(Jeremiah 29:11).*

*"This is what the L*ORD *says—your Redeemer, the Holy
One of Israel: 'I am the L*ORD *your God, who teaches
you what is best for you, who directs you in the way
you should go'" (Isaiah 48:17).*

I was watching a show on television the other day when one of the stars of the show asked a young lady what she wanted to be and how she saw herself in the future. Her response was, "I want to be an influencer." At first, I had no idea what she meant by that. I was equally baffled when the host replied in an enthusiastic, "Well, good for you!"

Then I remembered one of our pastor's comments during a recent sermon. "People believe you are obscure unless you do something spectacular. But as Christians our identity is not in what we do, but it is in who God says we are." As Christians we should all be "influencers." Jesus told us in Mark 16:15–16: *"Go into all the world and preach the gospel to all creation. Whoever believes and is baptized will be saved, but whoever does not believe will be condemned."* This command is not only for the lady who sits next to you in church or the young man in Sunday school. This command is for **all of us**. We need to be influencers in every circle of people we belong to.

The contemporary Christian music group called Casting Crowns sings a song called "Already There." In this song, the lead male singer tells how he looks forward to going to heaven where he will stand before Jesus, and together they will look back over his life Then he will see how all the pieces fit together to make sense. He has so many questions now, but he knows he will see how it all worked together when he gets to heaven with Jesus.

When we plan our future, one of the most important questions we should ask ourselves is, "Is my name in the book of life" (Revelation 20:12)? If not, it doesn't matter how many people we've influenced here on earth. God will not be impressed. His prerequisite to spending eternity with Him in heaven and having our name in the book of life is accepting Jesus as our Savior, the perfect sacrifice for our sins. When we have done this, one day we will stand before Jesus and look back over our lives to see how He connected the many pieces of our lives on earth. If we have not accepted Jesus' sacrifice on our behalf to wash away our sins, then we will still stand before Jesus, the Judge. He will judge our lives and see our sins, and our sins will condemn us. *"For the wages of sin is death, but the gift of God is eternal life in Christ Jesus our Lord"* (Romans 6:23).

Plan of Action

1. How are you doing as an "influencer" for Christ? Are you sharing the Gospel in your circles of influence? Are you living the gospel? This is a life-or-death message for your family, friends, and acquaintances.

2. We influence people not only by what we say but also by how we live. As professing Christians, we are judged by the world around us. Does our behavior match up with who we say we are—Christ followers who are led by the Holy Spirit?

3. Write out how your life is different because of Christ. How has your life changed? How did God's Word influence and encourage you? I pray God will give you the opportunity to share your salvation story with someone this week. Look for the opportunity and take it in faith that God will change a person's life.

Prayer

Lord, although the title of "influencer" is the buzz word now. You told us two thousand years ago that You wanted us to be influencers for Your Kingdom. Please open our eyes to see when You have opened an opportunity for us to walk into. Give us the courage and words to offer life to those You place in our path. Please help us to live according to Your direction in Your Word, the Bible. We also trust that when You lead us to share Your saving grace with a person, You will bless the listener with the ability and desire to understand Your message. We love You, Lord. Help us to trust You in our daily lives wherever You place us. In Jesus' name. Amen.

JEALOUSY

Scripture Reading: Galatians 5:16–26

"The acts of the sinful nature are obvious: sexual immorality, impurity and debauchery; idolatry and witchcraft; hatred, discord, jealousy, fits of rage, selfish ambition, dissensions, factions and envy; drunkenness, orgies, and the like" (Galatians 5:19–21a).

Do you see that jealousy and envy are listed among what we might consider extremely sinful behaviors? God ranks jealousy right up there. We are not to be jealous or envious, and we are not to covet other people's family or belongings (Deuteronomy 5:21).

The other day, I was putting on lipstick, and the Lord reminded me of when I was in the fifth grade. That was the first time that I remember being jealous of someone. A new girl moved into our community, and she had the most perfect rosebud lips. Of course, at that age I didn't know that term. I did know that she had perfectly shaped lips, and she was also pretty. The boys in my school were all abuzz about her.

Regretfully, because I was jealous of her, I didn't welcome her to our town. I did my best to ignore her. As I look back at that time, I am glad that most of the girls treated her with generous hospitality. But when I went home and looked in the mirror, I tried to make my lips look like hers. Naturally, that didn't work. If you look at my photo, you will see that God chose to give me very, very small lips. My sisters and I laugh with each other about the fact that God gave them beautiful lips and nails, while God chose to give me great hair. I love the way *The Living Bible* states Isaiah 45:9a and 11–12:

> *"Woe to the man who fights with his Creator. Does the pot argue with its maker? Does the clay dispute with him who forms it. . .. Jehovah, the Holy One of Israel, Israel's Creator, says: "What right have you to question what I do? Who are you to command me concerning the work of my hands? I have made the earth and created man upon it. With my hands I have stretched out the heavens and commanded all the vast myriads of stars."*

The point here is that God created each of us uniquely, and unless we are identical twins, we are all different, and even twins have their own personalities, likes, dislikes, and expressions. God made us different on purpose, and He has plans for our individual lives just the way He made us. I am sure that you are familiar with Jeremiah 29:11, *"'For I know the plans I have for you,' declares the LORD, 'plans for welfare and not for evil, to give you a future and a hope'"* (ESV). When we know that God loves each of us and wants only the best for us, there is really no reason for envy or jealousy. He has a call on each of our lives just the way He created us. We are important to Him. When we see a special treat that our neighbor might have or an award that one of our associates receive, we should rejoice with them for their blessing. It will even make us feel better if we congratulate them sincerely or simply be happy for them.

When I think of my fifth grade experience with jealousy, I think of a song that Frank Sinatra sang. One of the lines in *My Way* is "Regrets? I've had a few. But then again, too few to mention." Is there really anyone who can look over his or her life and say he/she has too few regrets to mention? I've had more than a few regrets of my choices and my behavior in my life. One regret is that I could have been friendlier to that new girl in town.

Today, I am immeasurably grateful to know that God continues "to grow me up" with the knowledge that He loves me even though I don't have rosebud lips.

Plan of Action

1. Can you think of anyone that you are jealous of? Ask the Lord's forgiveness. Now try to see that person's positive behaviors for which you can rejoice for them. Ask God to help you remove that jealous feeling, and ask Him to help you appreciate this person instead of feeling jealous of him or her.

2. Do you have a neighbor or coworker who has something that you want? Is the resulting feeling jealousy? Confess that to God and ask His forgiveness. Ask Him to help you get past the jealous feeling and help you to be sincerely happy for their achievement.

Prayer

Lord, forgive me for ever feeling jealous of anyone. Please remind me that You have made me exactly as You want and that You love me the way I am. Help me to rejoice in the way I am made and not to want to look like anyone else. In Psalm 75:6–7, You tell us that no one, no matter where they are from, can exalt a man. Only You bring one down and exalt another. Therefore, if someone else gets the promotion we wanted, we need to realize that was not in Your plan for our lives. In the same way, if we see someone who is extremely handsome or beautiful, we should praise You for creating such a beautiful human being. Lord, You know this will be impossible for me without Your help. I trust You will encourage me along the way. You have blessed me so very much. I am ashamed that I ever feel less or left out. Thank You, Lord, for my many blessings and for giving me life in Christ in whose name we pray. Amen.

JELLYBEANS

Scripture Reading: Ephesians 1:18–22

"I keep asking that the God of our Lord Jesus Christ, the glorious Father, may give you the Spirit of wisdom and revelation, so that you may know him better"
(Ephesians 1:17).

First of all, if you haven't read the Scripture Reading above, you must. If you don't have time right now, please come back to it sometime later today or tomorrow. What a wonderful prayer that Paul was praying for the Ephesians, and today because of the Holy Spirit, he prays for us. One year ago, our Ladies' Bible study chose the book of Ephesians for our summer study. A few weeks into our study, one of the ladies refreshed us all by observing that it was such a practical book which is applicable immediately to our lives today. It is indeed practical, and we are privileged to have it available for us to read. Through Paul's letter to the Ephesians, the Holy Spirit reminds us that we who believe have incomparably great power and mighty strength. With that power God raised Christ from the dead, and God tells us that power is for us.

The God who created the universe and everyone and everything in it had a conversation with the Old Testament character Job where He asked him where he was when He was creating the world (Job 38–41). These chapters are great to help us realize a bit of God's all-encompassing power. He created us, and He wants us to know that He is able to handle our businesses, our money, our families, our lives. He wants us to come to Him in prayer and lay our needs before him. Sometimes, when we pray, we ask for jellybeans when God wants to give us the candy factory. One of our pastors explained, "Our problem is not that we ask too much of God, but that we ask so little because we think so little of what He is able to do."

When I first discovered that God was with me everywhere I went, I loved talking to Him while I drove my car. I scheduled my life so I could wake up early and read the Bible, which I had just understood was His Word for me. I allowed myself thirty minutes for soaking up as much of His Word as possible. Then I had to drag myself away, so I could get ready for my forty-five-minute drive to the school where I taught French and English. During my drive, I prayed for the school administrators, the other teachers, and my students. I always reminded God (but really, I was reminding myself) that He had to do the teaching. I didn't know the needs of each student, but He did. I was trusting Him to do the work that was needed through me. I loved that drive. It was a wonderful blessing to have a time with just God and me.

If you read *Lord, It's Time for Just You and Me, Book 2*, you will remember the day the Lord told me to take Lindy, one of my students, out of her first-hour class to tell her that He loved her. I spent practically the rest of the forty-five-minute ride explaining to Him why that wouldn't work. Of course, it did work, and He touched a young girl that day in a way none of us could have imagined.

One reason I love writing is because when I am writing, I am in constant conversation with God. He gives me the idea and then He reminds me of Scriptures that I need to use. There are also times when He wants me to be still and wait for Him to show me what He wants me to write. I am privileged that He gives me such gifts, but no more than you. He loves you and me, and He loves to commune with you and me. First Thessalonians 5:16–18 instructs us to *"Be joyful always; pray continually; give thanks in all circumstances, for this is God's will for you in Christ Jesus."* We know that whenever God gives us instruction to do something, He will help us do it. God, we want to be joyful always. We want to pray continually and to give thanks in all circumstances because it is Your will for us. Please help us to do this.

Plan of Action

1. I learned early as I was growing up in my faith that if I was concerned about something, He wanted me to bring it before Him in prayer. Therefore, when we decided to buy our first house, He had me list everything I wanted in that house. Of course, He graciously led us to a house that had all I wanted and more. As I look back at that first house, I realize that it was small; but I didn't think that at the time because it was what we needed in the neighborhood where we were supposed to be. As our lives involved more interaction and ministry to people, our homes took on new looks. With His grace I have continued to list our needs in our homes, as I saw them, every time He has moved us, and I have loved every one of our homes. *"Ask and it will be given to you"* (Matthew 7:7a). Let Him be glorified in every part of your life. Ask for the candy factory all to His glory.

2. I want to balance out the candy factory prayer with this caution. James 4:3 states: *"When you ask, you do not receive, because you ask with the wrong motives, that you may spend what you get on your pleasures."* That doesn't nullify Matthew 7:7–11. God wants His best for us. Consequently, if we ask for something that is not in His will for us, He will not give it to us. I have been told that God has three answers to our prayers: yes, no, and not yet.

Prayer

Lord, only You know what is best for us. Your Word promises us that when we don't know what to pray, the Holy Spirit will give us the words and directions. Help us not to limit You by our own small vision of You. Let us discern between our own greed and our desire to ask what You truly want for us. Help us to always ask for the candy factory with the faith You give us by Your grace, to Your glory, in Jesus' name. Amen. P.S. Thank You, Lord.

JENNIE

Scripture Reading: James 2:1–4

"Therefore, as God's chosen people, holy and dearly loved, clothe yourselves with compassion, kindness, humility, gentleness and patience. . . . And over all these virtues put on love, which binds them all together in perfect unity" (Colossians 3:12, 14).

I have a friend whom I will call Jennie. She has held some admirable positions in her life, positions that could have easily gone to her head considering the importance of her status. But if you were to meet her, you would never know she held such significance because she would greet you as though you were one of the most important people in her life. She has been a fundraiser for many groups, one of which is a university. My husband and I have attended those money-raiser. I am always in awe of how she treats a brand-new freshman at the university with as much warmth, tenderness, and zeal as she treats the wealthiest of donors. It seems that she actually cares about everyone the Lord puts in her path. I say, "it seems" because I can't imagine that could be true of *every* person God places before her. But I have observed her for many years, and I have never seen her behave unkindly to anyone. When she asks a question, she looks in the eyes of each person and then patiently, intently listens to the answer. She keeps her attention on that one person even though there is usually a lot of activity going on around her. What a blessing she is! I am honored to know her. She is a remarkable role model. I want to be like her.

She lives just as the Holy Spirit instructs in 1 Corinthians 16:14: *"Do everything in love."* When I read 1 Corinthians 13:4–7, I see Jennie interacting with each person at an event.

> *Love is patient, love is kind. It does not envy, it does not boast, it is not proud. It is not rude, it is not self-seeking, it is not easily angered, it keeps no record of wrongs. Love does not delight in evil but rejoices with the truth. It always protects, always trusts, always hopes, always perseveres.*

Jennie makes each person, regardless of his or her station in life, feel as though he or she is the most important person at the event. Then I am reminded that her approach to each individual is just as James wrote in James 2:1–4. We are not to treat a wealthy, powerful, popular, or prestigious person differently than we treat a poor or seemingly powerless person. Each person is one of God's creations and important to Him.

Plan of Action

1. Let's review our lives. How have we treated people that we have met at fund raisers? At the grocery store? At the hairdresser's salon? At university open houses? At hotels with housecleaners, bellmen, busboys, and so on?

2. Let's decide today to love our neighbor as ourselves, to put on *"compassion, kindness, humility, gentleness and patience"* (Colossians 13:12b), and to *"put on love"* (Colossians 3:14) as we interact with the people God places in our path.

Prayer

Lord, how sweet and wise of You to tell us to love those who enter our lives. You tell us in Romans 5:5 that You have poured out Your love into our hearts by the Holy Spirit. You will help us love others as we are supposed to. Please do help us to behave as gentlemen and gentlewomen, pouring out Your love on others. What a gracious and loving God You are. And Lord, I ask that You continue to bless Jennie. Thank You for allowing me to know her, and thank You for the many Jennies in our lives. I praise You for them, and I pray all of this in my beloved Jesus' name. Amen.

JESUS IS SAVING A SEAT FOR YOU

Scripture Reading: John 14:1–7

"All the days ordained for me were written in your book before one of them came to be" (Psalm 139:16b).

We attend a very large church in Southwestern Florida. The pastors' messages are excellent and straight from the Bible. For this reason, on Sundays, we leave our home early enough to have our preferred seating area in the sanctuary. Even though we usually arrive twenty-five minutes before the worship service begins, sometimes our usual spot has evidence that someone is saving those seats. On top of the seats may be a message like "Saved for the greeters" or "Saved for the welcome desk people." Or people may have put their belongings on the seats to tell us that they are saving those seats for other friends or family. Consequently, we move on in search of other seats.

We are used to this scenario because we have been members of this church for years. Even though we are not surprised by our having to search for different seats, we are a bit discouraged by all the "saved seats." It occurred to me that if we, long-time members of the church, are a bit put out about all the saved seats, a visitor might feel quite discouraged by that. Many years ago, in one of the smaller churches where we were members, I heard that an elderly lady, who had sat in the same seat every Sunday for years, arrived and found visitors were sitting in her seat. She told them they had to move because they were in her seat. Yikes!

The wonderful news is that Jesus is saving a seat for us. We won't have to search for a vacant seat, and we won't arrive one minute before we should. Neither will we be late. We will arrive at His appointed time, and He'll have a seat saved especially for you and for me too.

Plan of Action

1. Let's make it a point to welcome people to our church. If your church is quite large as is ours, I find it useful to say, "I don't believe we have met yet. My name is Cheryl, and this is my husband, Bill." By starting with an introduction, you aren't assuming that the people you don't recognize are visitors or regular attendees.

2. If there comes a time when we save seats for friends or family, let's remember to be kind when we explain that the seats are saved. Sometimes, we are so quick to blast the people as though they are going to whisk in and take the saved seats that it comes out rudely. We can kindly say, "I am sorry, but these seats are saved for my family."

Prayer

Father, You know our thoughts here. We want to welcome people to our church and extend Your love to them. Yet there are times when we want to save seats for friends or family, and that may mean that we will have to direct people away from seats they thought they would have. Please help us to redirect people kindly and warmly, so they are not discouraged. Thank You for saving a seat for us. We love You so very much, Lord. Thank You for loving us. In Jesus' name. Amen.

JONAH

Scripture Reading: Jonah

"The LORD is gracious and compassionate, slow to anger and rich in love. The LORD is good to all; he has compassion on all he has made" (Psalm 145:8–9).

In my Christian journey, God has called me to speak at a variety of gatherings, and I knew He had a specific message in mind that He wanted delivered. As I prepared and even as I delivered His message, I knew that only God could open the heart and mind of each listener to receive His message.

Now let's look at Jonah. He did all he could to avoid delivering God's message to Nineveh. When God finally lassoed him to give the "repent or die message" to them, I wonder if Jonah delivered it with an "attitude"? Do you know what I mean? Since Jonah fiercely disliked the people of Nineveh, he may have been a bit sassy as he relayed God's message. Considering the response of the Ninevites, Jonah's delivery was effective because they did repent, and God spared them from the destruction that He had threatened to bring upon them (Jonah 3:10). As I said before, only God can open the heart and mind of the listener.

Have you ever wondered why the Lord chose Jonah? Why does the Lord choose any of us? God wants us to grow up spiritually, and there are lots of ways He arranges for that growth. When He told Jonah to go to Nineveh, He was not only giving the Ninevites the opportunity to change their evil ways, but God was also working on Jonah. The Lord had lots of people He could have chosen. But He chose Jonah. He needed a lesson in obedience.

Sometimes, God tells us to do something we don't want to do. This was Jonah's problem. Foolishly, he thought that if he got himself far away from Nineveh, God might let him off the hook. Jonah must have forgotten that no matter where he was, God was there too (Psalm 139:7–12). Obviously, running away didn't work. Jonah went through a couple of frightening experiences before he relented and obeyed God's direction. Jonah knew firsthand about God's willingness to forgive because God forgave Jonah and had commanded the huge fish to vomit him out of its stomach onto dry land (Jonah 2:10). Yet Jonah still didn't want God to forgive the Ninevites. Did you read what Jonah said when God spared the Ninevites? *"I knew that you are a gracious and compassionate God, slow to anger and abounding in love, a God who relents from sending calamity. Now, LORD, take away my life, for it is better for me to die than to live"* (Jonah 4:2b–3). Jonah, you want to die because God compassionately spared a city from destruction! Let's look at how God not so long ago preserved your life by having the large fish vomit you out of its stomach. REALLY, JONAH?!

The point here is that God can and will use whomever and whatever to convey His message to His beloved. Do you remember in Numbers 22:21–39 when God spoke to Balaam through the donkey he was riding? In 1 Samuel 3, the Lord spoke directly to Samuel. God gave Peter a vision to let him know he was supposed to share the gospel with Gentiles (Acts 10:1–23). Do you remember that God spoke to Paul when he was on the road to Damascus (Acts 9:1–

18)? Have you gone to church struggling with some problem, and the pastor's message seemed as though he had you in mind as he presented it? Well, the pastor may not have known your dilemma, but God did, and He was speaking to you through the pastor. Yes, God can use whomever and whatever to convey His message.

Another point is that while it may seem that the Lord is only working on the receivers of the message, we know that He is also working on the message giver. Just as God wanted the Ninevites to turn from their evil ways to obediently follow Him, He also wanted Jonah to obey when He told him to do something. Jonah was a prophet, and prophets were to obey and present God's message.

Plan of Action

1. We all have opportunities to speak to people every day. Let's be sure that we use words and actions that honor our Lord.

2. Whenever the Lord gives us an audience, we want to obediently speak for Him. First Peter 3:15 says, *"But in your hearts set apart Christ as Lord. Always be prepared to give an answer to everyone who asks you to give the reason for the hope that you have. But do this with gentleness and respect."*

Prayer

Father, I love the fact that You are always in control of my life, and You are at work refining me. Please help me to be ready to give a reason for the hope I have because of You. I ask You to help me always to be gentle and respectful as I share You with others. I also ask that You to align my will with Yours. I want to obey You now and forever. Thank You for Your compassion on all You have made, and that includes everyone who is reading this prayer and me too. You are awesome, Lord! I pray in Jesus' name. Amen.

JUDGING

Scripture Reading: Matthew 7:1–5

"It's easy to see a smudge on your neighbor's face and be oblivious to the ugly sneer on your own" (Matthew 7:4 MSG).

As my husband and I were going to church one Sunday, I looked out my window and thought, "Oh my. That car needs to be washed!" Then I realized it was our car that needed to be washed. I was all kinds of self-righteous until I realized that I was looking through our own dirty window! Of course, I immediately thought of the Scripture quoted above, and I was humbled.

People have used this Scripture to apply to any kind of judgment that we might give, and that doesn't match the instruction found in the rest of God's Word. Over and over in the Bible, we are warned to distinguish between truth and lies, Scripture and folklore, true and false prophets, right and wrong. Consequently, it might help us to distinguish between fact and error if we were to ask ourselves what we are comparing the teaching against. If the teaching is not in agreement with the Bible, be assured that we can judge it as erroneous or false. However, we don't want to rail against the speaker like a wrecking ball. That will not be helpful. We do want to approach the person with respect, grace, and reason, armed with God's Word.

When there is not a legitimate reason to judge the person or his message, yet you find yourself judging and objecting, it might be helpful to ask yourself why you are quick to judge this person. Perhaps you are jealous of the attention the speaker is getting. Or maybe you are afraid that he will take away from your "ministry." For example, we lived in two cities where, because of a problem in one church, the people in our church were rejoicing because it meant that people would leave that church and join ours. Instead of rejoicing when one church has a problem, every church member of every other church in the city should pray for the church that is having difficulties. There are more than enough unchurched people who need the truth, love, and compassion of His body. We don't need to be church member "stealing."

Just as I realized I was at fault judging the other person's car as dirty when it was really ours, we will sometimes have to judge people, circumstances, and doctrine. As Christians, we want to be sure our judgment is because the Holy Spirit within us has sent us an "alert," and not because of our trying to grandstand at the cost of others.

Plan of Action

1. Think about a time when you made a judgment based on an incorrect first impression. This is a good time to remind ourselves to be careful not to jump to conclusions before we have facts on which to base them.

2. If we do find ourselves in a place where someone is teaching something as sound doctrine when clearly it is not, ask where they found that message in the Bible. If they respond that they are sure it is in the Bible, ask them to find the exact location and come back to the group with that information at the next meeting. Then follow up. Don't let this situation end with the possibility that the group may believe that a teaching is true when it is not. But remember to act with grace and respect. The person may not know they are incorrect. They may just be repeating something they have heard for years and have taken it as truth.

Prayer

My Lord and my God, You want Your children to know the Truth without error. Give us discernment to know when we should question and when we should judge. Help us not to be too quick to judge and still not to allow false doctrine to be spread. We can only do this with Your help, and we are grateful knowing that You will guide us. We love You, Lord, and we pray in Jesus' name. Amen.

Note: I have found *Who Are You to Judge?* by Erwin W. Lutzer to be a valuable resource on this topic.

THE LAMB OF GOD

Scripture Reading: Exodus 12

"The next day John saw Jesus coming toward him and said, 'Look, the Lamb of God, who takes away the sin of the world'" (John 1:29).

In my first book, *Lord, It's Time for Just You and Me,* I wrote a devotional called "God's Favor," where I recounted the story about God sending an angel to the shepherds to announce Christ's birth. Then in *Lord, It's Time for Just You and Me, Book 3,* I wrote about Christ the Good Shepherd. In that devotional, I wrote about how God, our Father, chose shepherds to be the first to hear the announcement of the birth of the Good Shepherd, Jesus.

Up to now I had not recognized another significance of God sending the announcement of His Son's birth to shepherds. Maybe you have seen it all along. But in case you haven't understood it or heard it preached, here we go.

These shepherds may have supplied lambs for the Jews in temple sacrifices according to Numbers 28:1–10. We also find references to sacrificing lambs in Exodus 12 where we read about the Passover. Then we read about the Israelites sacrificing lambs as sin offerings in Exodus 29:38–43. Now we see these shepherds who spend their days taking care of the sheep: keeping them safe from predators, feeding them, moving them from one place to another, and so on. God gave these same shepherds a special invitation to see His Son, who is the Son of Man, the Son of God, our Creator, our Savior, and yes, the Lamb of God who will be sacrificed for our sins.

Plan of Action

1. Jesus, the perfect Lamb of God, allowed Himself to be killed as a sacrifice for our sins—yours and mine. Spend some time worshiping and thanking our beloved Jesus.

2. Remember that the God of the world loves you, even though He knows the worst about you. You are important to Him, and He has a purpose for your life (Psalm 138:8). I pray you are serving Him as He has called you. If you are unsure of His call on your life, ask Him to reveal what He wants you to do. Matthew 7:7 reads, "*Ask and it will be given to you; seek and you will find; knock and the door will be opened to you.*" He loves you and has a purpose for your life that is good for you and others.

Prayer

Lord, I thank You for loving me, for creating me, and for sending Jesus to die in my place. He is perfect, and I am not, yet You love me. Please keep me in the center of Your will. Help me to hear Your voice clearly and to obey. Thank You, my precious Lamb of God, for dying to take away my sins. Please help me in the future to recognize when I have sinned, to confess it immediately, and to accept Your forgiveness. I love You, Jesus, and I pray in Your name. Amen.

LAZARUS, COME OUT!

Scripture Reading: John 11:17–44

"Jesus called in a loud voice, 'Lazarus, come out!' The dead man came out, his hands and feet wrapped with strips of linen, and a cloth around his face. Jesus said to them, 'Take off the grave clothes and let him go"
(John 11:43b–44).

In case you are not familiar with this story, let me provide a bit of background for you. Jesus was close friends with Lazarus and his two sisters, Mary and Martha. In fact, He loved them, and they loved Jesus (John 11:5). He received word that Lazarus was ill but instead of rushing to see him, Jesus waited to go to Lazarus until he had been dead for four days. Jesus waited because He had a tremendous miracle in store for His beloved friends to witness.

When Jesus arrived at the tomb where Lazarus was buried, He asked the people to roll away the stone that closed off the tomb. Then Jesus says, *"Lazarus, come out!"* And out he came covered in burial cloths. I have read in Bible commentaries that if Jesus had not addressed Lazarus specifically, many other dead people likely would have responded to the Creator by coming back to life and exiting their tombs. Doesn't that make you smile as you imagine that?

Where were you when Jesus called you by name? Where were you when He gave you new life in Him? I was in seventh grade in a worship service when I realized I had a heavenly Father who really loved me and gave up His Son to die in my place so that I could be His daughter. Though it took years for that to sink in, I can still see that young me sitting in the pew in awe of and supremely comforted by such love.

Just as Jesus called Lazarus out from his grave to give him life, He has called each of us to go from death to life—eternal life with Him. Although we weren't physically in a tomb, we were the walking dead until Christ called our names and gave us new life. The people around us may not have known it. Perhaps we didn't know that we were dead until Christ called our name. Jesus said in John 3:3 *"Truly, truly, I say to you, unless one is born again he cannot see the kingdom of God"* (ESV). He has spoken to each of us and said: "(Write your name here) _____, come out! Come join Me." So the next time you read John 11:17–44, you can rejoice with Jesus that He called you from your tomb and gave you new life.

Plan of Action

1. How are you serving Him now that He has given you new life in Christ? Are you involved in a good Bible-believing church?

2. You have heard the saying, "When He calls you, He also equips you." When you became a member of His family, He blessed you with spiritual gifts. Those gifts are given to serve His body, the church. Paul instructed Timothy to *"fan into*

flame" the gift God had given him (2 Timothy 1:6). If you are not yet using your gifts, look for where God wants you to serve. It is not arrogance to recognize your gifts and put them to use. How can receiving His gifts make us arrogant when we didn't do anything to deserve them? If someone gives you a book as a gift, do you become arrogant because of the gift? Of course not!

3. Are there people in your circle of friends who have not yet heard Jesus calling their names? Ask God to open their ears to hear His call.

Prayer

Father, first of all, thank You for calling me out of death and into life with You. Help me to fulfill Your purpose in my life. Lord, I ask that You open up my friends' ears to hear You call their names, and then please help them to follow You in their new lives. If You want to use me in their lives, open my ears and eyes to serve however You desire. I love You, Lord. In Jesus' name. Amen.

LIFE PRESERVER

Scripture Reading: John 14:15–31

"Jesus said to her, 'I am the resurrection and the life. The one who believes in me will live, even though they die; and whoever lives by believing in me will never die. Do you believe this?'" (John 11:25–26).

If you saw a person drowning, and you had a life preserver, you would throw it to the person drowning. Of course, that person would grab it to save his life. He wouldn't ask, "Now are you a premillennialist or postmillennialist?" Or "Do you believe Jonah was actually swallowed by a whale? Or is that just a story to make a point?" Or "Are you a Baptist or a Presbyterian?" Trust me on this: The drowning person will gratefully receive the life preserver and ask no questions.

I would like for us to consider this the next time we feel we need to criticize others who may view parts of the Bible differently than we do. Let's do less nitpicking with each other. Our biggest question as we look at other denominations should be: How do they treat the trinity: Father, Jesus the Son, and the Holy Spirit? We need to remember that the most important thing we need to know is that our heavenly Father sent His Son, Christ, the Messiah, who came to this earth to teach us, and then He gave His life as the perfect sacrifice for our sins (John 3:16). Christ died so we can live with Him in heaven forever. Once we accept Him as our Savior, we are blessed to have the Holy Spirit in us to remind us of what Jesus taught when He was here (John 14:26).

As Christians we are walking around with God's Living Word and the Holy Spirit inside us, and we need to be ready to extend this life preserver to those around us who need it without fear that we don't know enough. When we see those who are lost, look on them with compassion. With the Holy Spirit and because of Christ's sacrifice, you have what they need. If God presents the opportunity, offer His life preserver with an abundance of love and without fear.

Plan of Action

1. Ask the Lord to give you the opportunity to offer the life preserver you have to another person.

2. You might want to write out what you would like to say when you offer the life preserver. By doing that you will have it in mind and won't be caught off guard. But even if you have the opportunity before you have "perfected" what you want to say, trust the Holy Spirit to speak through you. He is trustworthy. ☺

Prayer

Father, please help me to see every opportunity You present for me to share Your very good news about Christ and all He has done for us sinners. Please give me the confidence to speak. Help me to be gentle and kind while I speak Your Truth. I trust You, and I love You. In Jesus' name I pray. Amen.

THE MAJESTY OF GOD

Scripture Reading: Luke 9:37–43

"*And all were astonished at the majesty of God*" (Luke 9:43 ESV).

Have you been astonished at the majesty of God? Have you seen a stunning sunset? Have you seen a beautiful bird in flight? Have you been in awe of the birth of a baby? Have you been moved by the music made by an orchestra or even a solo violinist or a vocalist? Have you relished the taste of a crisp apple? These are just glimpses of His majesty. We are moved by them, and as Christians, we know who creates all these wonders and we give Him thanks and praise for His mighty works. "*Bless the Lord, O my soul! O Lord my God, you are very great! You are clothed with splendor and majesty*" (Psalm 104:1 ESV). Please ponder Hebrews 1:3:

> *He is the radiance of the glory of God and the exact imprint of his nature, and he upholds the universe by the word of his power. After making purification for sins, he sat down at the right hand of the Majesty on high.*

We know this is speaking of the Lord Jesus. There will be a time when every person will be astonished at the majesty of God:

> *And I heard every creature in heaven and on earth and under the earth and in the sea, and all that is in them, saying, "To him who sits on the throne and to the Lamb be blessing and honor and glory and might forever and ever."*
>
> —Revelation 5:13 ESV

I pray that all our families and friends appreciate and acknowledge the majesty of God in their lives on this side of heaven. *"But I, when I am lifted up from the earth, will draw all people to myself"* (John 12:32).

Now think about this: *"So God created mankind in his own image, in the image of God he created them, male and female he created them"* (Genesis 1:27). Do you wonder what God looks like? God created men and women in His image. Because we are fallible human beings who need Him in every part of our lives, we find it hard to believe that we are made in His image. Nevertheless, His Word says that God created us in His image. *"And we, who with unveiled faces all reflect the Lord's glory, are being transformed into his likeness with ever-increasing glory, which comes from the Lord, who is the Spirit"* (2 Corinthians 3:18). The Holy Spirit is at work transforming us to become more and more like Christ.

If you ever hear a voice saying, "You are nothing! Who do you think you are?" You can answer, "I am a child of God. I am made in His image, and He loves me and takes care of me." Then read the Scriptures I have placed in this devotional. Our God is always with us, and He is always transforming us to be more and more like Christ. Praise His holy name!

Plan of Action

1. Ask the Lord to help you keep your priorities in line with His.
2. Ask Him to help you recognize when you are sidetracked by insignificant or minor distractions during your quiet time with Him, and ask Him to help you stay focused on Him and His Word.

Prayer

Lord, You know that my quiet time with You is important to me, and I know it is important to You too. Please help me to guard our precious time together, and keep me from being distracted. I desire to submit to and see more of Your Majesty. I love You, Lord, and I thank You that You love me. In Jesus' name. Amen.

> "God not only loves you very much but also has put his hand on you for something special" (1 Thessalonians 1:4 MSG).

> "Who is like you, O Lord, among the gods? Who is like you, majestic in holiness, awesome in glorious deeds, doing wonders" (Exodus 15:11 ESV)?

> "Yours, O Lord, is the greatness and the power and the glory and the victory and the majesty, for all that is in the heavens and in the earth is yours. Yours is the kingdom, O Lord, and you are exalted as head above all" (1 Chronicles 29:11 ESV).

> "O Lord, our Lord, how majestic is your name in all the earth" (Psalm 8:9 ESV)!

*"Bless the L*ORD*, O my soul! O L*ORD *my God, you are very great! You are clothed with splendor and majesty"* (Psalm 104:1 ESV).

"On the glorious splendor of your majesty, and on your wondrous works, I will meditate" (Psalm 145:5 ESV).

"For we did not follow cleverly devised myths when we made known to you the power and coming of our Lord Jesus Christ, but we were eyewitnesses of his majesty. For when he received honor and glory from God the Father, and the voice was borne to him by the Majestic Glory, 'This is my beloved Son, with whom I am well pleased'" (2 Peter 1:16–17 ESV).

MAKE THE CALL

Scripture Reading: 1 Samuel 18:1–4

"Gracious words are a honeycomb, sweet to the soul and healing to the bones" (Proverbs 16:24).

My husband and I have been married for fifty-five years, and for fifty-two of those years we have mailed newsletters at Christmas to our friends and family. Because the Lord has moved us around a bit, we have a fairly long list of people with whom we want to stay in touch. For the first two years of our marriage, as we wrote our Christmas cards, we found we were writing practically the same thing on each card. Thus, the newsletter was born. We have an agreement with our family that our annual letter will be no longer than one page with no smaller than 10-point type.

This year we received a wonderful surprise in a newsy, three-page handwritten Christmas letter from a very close friend who lives in another state. In it she filled us in on their activities by giving a general overview of several years.

I was so touched that I decided to call four of our mutual friends. I knew that my husband and I were the only ones who had maintained contact with her. She had recorded enough significant points that I knew I had to call and read the letter to them. I was sure the other women would love to hear from our mutual friend. Consequently, when the busy Christmas season had passed, I called those four ladies and read the letter to them in January.

Those phone calls were a blessing all around. First of all, it had been years since I had spoken to each of these friends. All of us now live in different cities or states, and our forms of communication have been postal mail, email, or texts. Therefore, to talk with each friend gave us the opportunity to "catch-up" with each other. Two of them ended the call with, "You have made my day!" God used this letter to bless the writer and the recipient, as well as our mutual friends. All praise to God!

Plan of Action

Spend a few moments and think of some of your dear friends who live in a different town or state and whose voice you haven't heard for a while. Consider giving them a call. Those of us who have "smart" phones do a variety of activities with them. We text, take photos, send icons, read our emails, and so on. I am asking you to use your phone for the purpose phones were originally intended. Call your friend. You will bless the recipient, and you will be blessed too.

Prayer

Lord, thank You for giving us dear friends. Remind us from time to time to call one of them and to allow ourselves to bathe in the friendship. Because of Jesus, we have many Christian family members. Nudge us to lavish our friends with love. We pray in our beloved Jesus' name. Amen.

MIRRORS

Scripture Reading: Ephesians 4:22–24

"So all of us who have had that veil removed can see and reflect the glory of the Lord. And the Lord—who is the Spirit— makes us more and more like him as we are changed into his glorious image"
(2 Corinthians 3:18 NLT).

As I aged, I have found that using a magnifying mirror is quite helpful when I am putting on makeup. The magnifying mirror helps me to see precisely how I am applying makeup, and sadly, it also magnifies the flaws in my face.

Aren't we grateful that people don't look at us with magnifying mirrors? Many of our flaws, both physical and behavioral, can go unseen. The amazing truth is that God sees all our flaws and loves us anyway. Thank You, Lord! In fact, every day since we accepted Jesus as our Savior, He has been at work in us to erase our behavioral flaws. Here is 2 Corinthians 3:18 as translated in the NIV Bible: *"And we all . . . are being transformed into his image with ever-increasing glory, which comes from the Lord, who is the Spirit."* He is perfect, and His work in us is better than plastic surgery. ☺

Plan of Action

1. As we live in Christ, we can rejoice knowing the truth of Philippians 1:6: *"And I am sure of this, that he who began a good work in you will bring it to completion at the day of Jesus Christ"* (ESV). He will not give up on us. We must not become discouraged when we mess up. Look into His Word; you may want to start with the book of Psalms. Many of the psalms are written by David who was being pursued by King Saul who wanted to kill him. Although threatened with death, David still knew he could trust the Lord to keep him safe.

2. As you go through your day, remember that we can be mirrors that brightly reflect the glory of the Lord. Don't you love that? I truly pray that as people look at me, they will see the glory of the Lord. I also pray that as I go through my day, that I honor Him in word and deed.

Prayer

Lord, as I said before, when people look at me, I want them to see Your glory in my countenance and in my deeds. Help me to represent You well. I also pray that when people see Your glory in me, they would be inclined to ask me why I am so full of love and peace. If You want to use me to draw others to You, I am willing. Thank You, Lord. All I am and all I do are to Your glory. I pray in Jesus' name. Amen.

MOTHER

Scripture Reading: Proverbs 31:10–31

"But the fruit of the Spirit is love, joy, peace, patience, kindness, goodness, faithfulness, gentleness, self-control" (Galatians 5:22–23 ESV).

My husband and I began our marriage at the same time that we began our professions. I was a beginning teacher, and my husband was a teaching assistant at the university where he was working on his PhD degree. Our income was meager. In fact, there were times when our food supply was down to just one can of beans. Interestingly, my mother would call on that particular night and say, "Cheryl, I made too much spaghetti for your dad and me. Could I bring some over for you?" Since we lived in the same small town as my parents, I could easily say, "Yes! Feel free to bring it over!" This happened several times. We had told no one about our lack of food. But mom was undoubtedly prompted by the Holy Spirit both to make an abundance of food and to offer the extra to us.

As I said, we lived in a small town of twenty-five hundred people. When someone was sick, my mother would take food to the family. That way, they could eat without bothering to prepare meals. When someone in the community died, Mom would take food to the family. And then with the sympathy card, she would include postage stamps because in those days, people wrote thank you notes to those who sent flowers or food. Mom wanted to save them from having one more thing to buy. As I read over Proverbs 31:10–31, I see Mom's wisdom, generosity, unselfishness, and hard work. Then when I read Galatians 5:22–23, which I have quoted above, I see that her life exhibited all of them.

In all my life, I only heard her say unkind words twice. One time was when Mom and Dad arrived home from a convention. Mom spoke with disdain about one of the ladies there who was flirting with my father. The other time was when she was commenting about several women's evening wear—the necklines were cut too low. I believe she was making sure I knew that was unacceptable as a proper young woman.

I remember Mom telling me about the times she had spoken unkindly to me when I was young; she said that when she went to bed in the evening, she would ask God to erase that from my memory. To this day, I don't remember her ever speaking unkindly to me. God answers prayers.

My husband refers to her as Saint Marcy because she answered unkind words with kindness and unkind behavior with generous grace. Oh yes, I must add that Mom loved my husband as if he were her own son.

Plan of Action

1. If your mother is still living and if she lives close to you, plan to meet her for lunch, and you pay for it.

2. If your mother is still living, write her a kind note or choose a sweet or funny card to send and let her know that you love and appreciate all she has given you.

3. If you tend to be critical of your mother, cast it away in the wind. She probably did the best she could. You need to forgive her and love her. The Holy Spirit can help you with that. Romans 5:5 tells us that God has poured His love into our hearts, and with His love, we can love others.

Prayer

Lord, I know that my mom was not perfect. No human being is. But from my perspective, she was very close to being perfect. Thank You for allowing my sisters and me to have such a mother. I pray for everyone whose mother was unkind or selfish or hateful. I know You can heal the wounds that they have caused. Please encourage the mothers who are reading this. We are not perfect, and yet You love us and are working all things for our good (Romans 8:28). I also ask that You bless those women who have not given birth to children but are mothers in Your call on their lives. Lord, You love us all and have our lives in Your hands. Indeed, Lord, Your grace is sufficient for all of us. Thank You, Father. I pray in Jesus' name. Amen.

MY FRIEND, JAN

Scripture Reading: Psalm 1:1–3

"'And you shall love the LORD your God with all your heart, with all your soul, with all your mind, and with all your strength.' This is the first commandment. And the second, like it, is this: 'You shall love your neighbor as yourself.' There is no other commandment greater than these" (Mark 12:30–31 NKJV).

I have a friend who is really very, very close to being perfect. She never says a critical or unkind word; she is totally selfless. She is a wonderful, encouraging lady not only to her friends but to others as well. You have certainly heard someone describe another as "simply glowing." Well Jan always "glows" with the beautiful radiance of the Holy Spirit. Many years ago, she and I sang in a ministry group. One time, one of the ladies wanted someone to listen to our music from what would be the audience's perspective, from in front of us, and Jan was chosen. As she listened, she had a peaceful, beautiful glow. When asked how we sounded, she answered, "Perfectly beautiful." I am sure that if we had asked someone else to listen, that person would have said, "You sound fine." I believe the difference was that Jan loved us like we are supposed to love one another, and she filtered everything about us through that love.

It seems to me that Jan flawlessly follows the commandments quoted above. She truly loves God and her neighbors, in this case, us. Notice that I wrote that it "seems to me." I realize that Jan is human, and as humans, we all sin (Romans 3:23). Nevertheless, she seems to exemplify one of God's near-perfect creations. She spends time in God's Word, and one of her spiritual gifts is intercessory prayer. She seems to be infused with joy.

I do know that if I were to tell her what I have written about her, she would laugh and say, "Oh, Cheryl, you don't know the real me." Jan, I believe I do. Today we live several hundred miles from each other. But I imagine if I were to ask the people who know her in the city where she now lives, they would say the same: Jan glows from the inside out with the beautiful radiance of the Holy Spirit, and yes, she is a nearly perfect human being.

Plan of Action

1. Do you have anyone like Jan in your life? If so, consider giving her a call or writing her a note to let her know what a blessing she is.

2. Can you think of a friend who could use a word of encouragement or perhaps a hug? Should you call him or her, or should you write a note? Be open to giving your Christian sisters and brothers a hug when you see them. I try to remember to hug widows and widowers. Not long after my mother became a widow, she told me that as a widow she rarely had physical touch from anyone. She really appreciated it when someone hugged her.

Prayer

Father, I thank You for creating all the "Jans" in our lives. As You know, they bless us in so many ways and one of those ways is exemplifying Your love for and care of us. I ask that You help us to be more like Jan with our love for one another. Help us to love without prejudice or judgments. Lord, please help us to love as You love. We know this is only possible by the power of the Holy Spirit. Thank You for sending Him to live in us. We love You, Lord, and we pray in Jesus' name. Amen.

ON CALL

Scripture Reading: 1 Samuel 3:1–10

"Then I heard the voice of the Lord saying, 'Whom shall I send? And who will go for us'" (Isaiah 6:8)?

I am sure you are familiar with the term "on call." These days, our doctors don't work seven days a week as they used to. When they have days off, there is a doctor who is "on call" for the medical practice. That means if you have a medical problem, you can call the "on-call" doctor to get help. Even our large church of fifteen hundred plus members has an "on-call" pastor. In a similar way, I want to be "on call" for our Lord. If He needs someone to encourage one of His beloved or to minister in any way, I want to be ready to go and do whatever He asks of me.

If you have read any of my devotionals, you know that I am very big on listening for God's voice when you need direction in your life. Most often you will hear Him as you read His Word. Sometimes, He will clearly speak to your mind. When you hear Him in your mind, remember that He will never ask or tell you to do anything that is contrary to His written Word, the Bible. Sometimes, He will speak through a friend, a Sunday School teacher, or a pastor. Often, He speaks through more than one just to confirm to you that His voice truly is His voice. Remember His Word in James 1:5: "*If any of you lacks wisdom, he should ask God, who gives generously to all without finding fault, and it will be given to him.*" That is God's Word telling you that if you need to figure something out, He is ready and willing to steer you in the right direction. Just ask Him.

Plan of Action

1. How ready are you to place yourself "on call" for the Lord? When He asks us to do a new thing, He will equip us to do it. He will walk with us each step of the way. We can trust Him. Remember He is able to keep the universe moving. He can handle anyone and any place where He sends us.

2. When the Holy Spirit asks me to do something I haven't done before, He is gracious to give me a picture in my mind of how it will all take place. All I have to do is follow the pattern He has set before me. As you obey Him in the small ways He leads you, He will give you bigger responsibilities. There are very few things in this world that can compare to the awe and joy you will experience as you walk into new places with Him.

Prayer

My Lord and my God, I am in awe of You. I am in awe that You would desire to communicate with me. I am in awe that You would use me in ministering to You loved ones here on this earth. Father, I pray that when you speak to me, I will hear clearly. Please give me the courage to walk in obedience to Your directions. I love You, Lord, and I am overwhelmed by the fact that You desire to use me and bless me. Thank You, Lord. It is in Jesus' name I pray. Amen.

OUR NEW LIFE

Scripture Reading: Acts 9:1–22

"Do not be conformed to this world, but be transformed by the renewal of your mind, that by testing you may discern what is the will of God, what is good and acceptable and perfect" (Romans 12:2 ESV).

"Now the Lord is the Spirit, and where the Spirit of the Lord is, there is freedom. And we all, with unveiled face, beholding the glory of the Lord, are being transformed into the same image from one degree of glory to another. For this comes from the Lord who is the Spirit" (2 Corinthians 3:17–18 ESV).

First, we are transformed when we recognize that we are sinful and need His forgiveness and help. Then by God's grace, He places His seal of ownership on us (Ephesians 1:13). We realize that His sacrifice washes away our sin. As we look back to the day when we accepted Christ, we can see how the Lord has changed us from the inside out and will continue to change us.

Once our new life begins, do we never sin again? Sadly, we will. But now we can confess that sin immediately and ask for forgiveness.

God is gracious to forgive us and wipe that sin off our life record (1 John 1:9). When you think of that sin in the future, dismiss it. God has already forgiven you. Satan will want you to wallow in your guilt, but God doesn't do that. He convicts you of the sin. You ask Him for forgiveness; He forgives you. That is that; it's done. If Satan continues to try to make you feel guilty because of your past sin, tell him, "That person is dead. I am a new creation." Second Corinthians 5:17 states, *"Therefore, if anyone is in Christ, he is a new creation. The old has passed away; behold, the new has come"* (ESV).

Plan of Action

1. Is there someone who seems so sinful that they seem beyond Christ's reach? Pray for them. Look at how God changed Saul, a Roman Jewish Pharisee who persecuted Christians, into the Apostle Paul, who wrote fourteen of the twenty-seven books of the New Testament.

2. Do you see parts of your life that don't exemplify Christ? Trust your life to Him. He can change you—all of you. Philippians 2:13 reads, *"For it is God who works in you to will and to act according to his good purpose."*

3. Bathe yourself in the fact that God loves you just as you are. Whatever changes need to be made, He will do with love by the Holy Spirit.

Prayer

What a gracious, loving Father You are! I know that You still do miracles because when You gave me new life, You gave my life purpose. I am grateful for the changes You are making in me, and I know that You will continue sharpen my skills and soften any harshness in me. Transform me to Your image. Sanctify me. I am Yours, and I love You. I pray in Jesus' name. Amen.

OUR RISEN LORD

Scripture Reading: Luke 24:1–50 and John 20:1–18

"For what I received I passed on to you as of first importance that Christ died for our sins according to the Scriptures, that he was buried, that he was raised on the third day according to the Scriptures, and that he appeared to Peter, and then to the Twelve. After that he appeared to more than five hundred of the brothers at the same time . . ."
(1 Corinthians 15:3–6a).

We see in Luke 24:1 that on the first day of the week, Mary Magdalene, Mary the mother of James, and Joanna went to the tomb where Jesus' body had been placed. The Scripture says they carried spices to prepare Jesus' body. There was an earthquake and *"an angel of the Lord"* (Matthew 28:2) rolled the stone away from the tomb where Jesus had lain. The sight of the angel terrified the guards so much that they *"shook and became like dead men"* (Matthew 28:3–4). The angel reassured the women that just as Jesus had said He would do, He had risen from the dead. The angel told them to go tell His disciples that Jesus was going ahead and would meet them in Galilee. When the women told the apostles, they didn't believe them. Peter and John ran to the tomb to see for themselves (John 20:3–9). It cracks me up that John makes a point of telling us that he arrived at the tomb first. In other words, they had raced each other there, and John won the race! They were Jesus' apostles, but they were still very human.

After seeing that indeed Jesus' body was no longer in the tomb, the disciples returned to their homes. But Mary Magdalene stayed at the tomb and wept. When she looked into the tomb, she saw two angels who asked her why she was crying. She told them that someone had taken her Lord away. She was still looking for His dead body. When she turned around, Jesus said, *"Woman, why are you crying?"* She didn't recognize Him until He said, *"Mary"* (John 20:15–16). Then she knew it was Jesus.

Later, two other disciples walked and talked with our risen Lord on the road to Emmaus, but they didn't recognize Him until He broke bread with them (Luke 24:13–32). They said in Luke 24:34 that Jesus had also appeared to Simon Peter.

Later, we find that although the disciples were behind a locked door, Jesus appeared before them and breathed on them saying, *"Receive the Holy Spirit"* (John 20:19–23). One week later, Jesus appeared before the disciples again and said, *"Peace be with you"* (John 20:26). During this visit He shows Thomas His hands and has him put his hand in His side because Thomas had said he wouldn't believe that the disciples had indeed seen the risen Christ until he could *"see the nail marks in his hands and put* [his] *finger where the nails were, and put* [his] *hand into his side"* (John 20:25). John tells us that he couldn't list all the many miraculous signs that Jesus did because they wouldn't fit in his book (John 20:30).

I love to read in John 21 about the time Jesus appeared on the Sea of Tiberias (Galilee). This was another instance when the disciples went fishing through the night but caught nothing. Then a man on the shore suggested that they throw their nets on the other side. Their catch was so large they couldn't haul them all in. At this point, John recognized that the man was Jesus. I smile again at John's wording: *"Then the disciple whom Jesus loved said to Peter, 'It is the Lord'"* (John 21:7)! *Do* you realize that you and I can refer to ourselves as the disciple whom Jesus loves? He does love you and me, you know? He died on the cross for us and then arose so that we can live with Him forever, for eternity.

Before Jesus returned to heaven, He told His disciples that the Father would send the Holy Spirit in Jesus' name who *"will teach you all things and remind you of everything I have said to you"* (John 14:26). With the Holy Spirit living in us, we always have God's help at hand. We don't have to pray that our heavenly Father or Jesus will come our way because He already is with us in the third person of the trinity: the Holy Spirit.

Plan of Action

1. What a wonder that our God loves us so much! He gave us His word and the Holy Spirit. He never leaves us alone. He is always available to protect, comfort, encourage, teach, and so much more. Whatever we do, we do it with Him and in His strength. Consider any task that is before you. You will not be doing it with your own strength but in His. Remember to thank Him and give Him the glory.

2. In every conversation, we have the Holy Spirit as a witness. James 1:19 cautions us *"My dear brothers, take note of this: Everyone should be quick to listen, slow to speak."* There are

several proverbs that have similar warnings. However, we see that *"the tongue of the righteous is choice silver"* (Proverbs 10:20). As we listen well, let's be sure that when we speak, our words are a blessing to those who are listening.

Prayer

Lord, as we read Your word, please make it real to us. Help us to see Your humor, Your beauty, Your direction. It is Your letter to us, and it is new every time we read it. Forgive us for approaching it as one more task to do for the day. Instead open our minds and hearts to see You in every word. You tell us that as we read Your word, we become wise. Give us wisdom as to when and how we should speak whether we are in a conversation, teaching, or preaching. Let our words be as silver to those around us, and let them nourish the listeners. We trust You with our lives, Lord. We pray in Jesus' name. Amen.

THE PARABLE OF THE RICH FARMER

Scripture Reading: Luke 12:13–21

*"As long as he sought the L*ORD*, God gave him success"*
(2 Chronicles 26:5b).

Many pastors have preached that money and wealth are not evil; it is our view of money and what we do with it that is either evil or good. If we worship our wealth and want to obtain more and more out of greed or a desire for power, that is evil. If God is who we worship, and He is in the driver's seat of how we use and even earn our money, it is merely a tool to make life better for others as well as for ourselves.

In Luke 12:16, Jesus describes a rich farmer whose ground produced a good crop. He asked himself where he would put his crops, and he decided he would tear down his barns and build bigger barns. Then he could take life easy, sit back and *"eat, drink, and be merry"* (Luke 12:19b). God calls the rich farmer a fool and tells him that he will die that very night. In addition, God asks him, *"Who will get what you have prepared for yourself?"* (Luke 12:20) We don't want to stop reading the Bible there because the next paragraph gives us the reason why God is not happy about this man's wealth. *"This is how it will be with anyone who stores up things for himself but is not rich toward God"* (Luke 12:21).

According to the Westminster Catechism, man's (and woman's) chief end is to glorify God and enjoy Him forever. As Christians, our main purpose is to glorify God in whatever we do (1 Corinthians 10:31), and we are blessed to be able to enjoy Him as well. Our God is our Father, and He loves us and loves to bless us. The rich farmer had left God out of his life. He was just building riches with no thought of how God would like him to use them. God may have even let him build more barns had he worked with Him. I remember reading the story of King Uzziah in 2 Chronicles 26:1–21. At the age of sixteen, Uzziah became King of Judah. The chapter describes his successes, and they were many! He reigned in Jerusalem for fifty-two years where he won wars, rebuilt towns and towers, had productive fields and vineyards, had a well-trained army of 307,500 men, and more The Holy Spirit had the author add this statement: *"As long as he sought the LORD, God gave him success"* (2 Chronicles 26:5b). Sadly, we learn in 2 Chronicles 26:16a *"But after Uzziah became powerful, his pride led to his downfall."* It's a very sad story with an important message. If you haven't read it, please do.

If we are living only to make more money and acquire more stuff, where will our money and stuff go when we die? It will go to someone who has not worked for it. Hopefully, it will go to people who will seek God as they use it. When I see people on television who have won the lottery, received Olympic medals, won the Super Bowl, or such, I always pray, "Lord, if they don't know You, please draw them to You." In a few days, weeks, or months, that success won't satisfy. Then they'll be off to chase a new goal. My preacher spoke of a condition called "arrival fallacy."

This is when people look at a future goal, and believe that when they reach that goal, they will be happy, fulfilled, and successful. Setting and reaching goals are good practices, but attained goals do not make a person happy, joyful, or satisfied forever. That is why many people strive for one "medal" after another.

As Christians we should devote our lives to seeking the Lord in all that we do. He loves to give us direction (Psalm 32:8). In fact, He loves us and wants His best for us. Who among us would not want to ask for His advice and direction when we know He loves us and wants the best for us? Satisfaction comes from knowing and serving our Lord. That feeling of fulfillment cannot be beat!

Plan of Action

1. When I was working on my MBA, studying textbooks and writing my thesis, I found myself thinking of what I would rather do than my classwork. I started making a list of activities on which I would embark once I had completed my degree. The day after I finished my classwork, I picked up that list and started doing the items I had listed one by one. It was great! I had a new purpose, a new goal. I believe this helped me to avoid that condition called "arrival fallacy." I knew He wanted me to get my MBA; but that was only one part of His plans for me. God always has lots for His children to do, and working for Him is beyond wonderful with new worlds for us to explore right around the corner. Life as a Christian should never be boring. Instead, it is an adventure.

2. If you are in the middle of a project, hand it over to Him. Ask Him for help. Then listen to what He says. Look for His direction. Working with Him is amazing! He brings life to even the humdrum.

Prayer

Father, I do not want to ever exercise my will as Uzziah did later in his life. Please keep me submitted to You and Your goals for all my days. Remind me that You have given me life to glorify and enjoy You forever. Remind me to use my gifts to bless You and Your people. Lord, I am humbled to think that You love me and want to be included in my life. Thank You. What a wonder You are. I pray in Your precious Son's name. Amen.

PERSPECTIVE

Scripture Reading: John 3

"But now, this is what the LORD says—he who created you, Jacob, he who formed you, Israel: 'Do not fear, for I have redeemed you; I have summoned you by name; you are mine.'" (Isaiah 43:1).

From time to time, I call members of my family "Sugar." Consequently, after I had called our grandson "Sugar" several times, he answered, "Hi, Hot Dog," or "Hi, Peanut Butter," or Hi, Tacos!" Then he would laugh. It took me a couple of FaceTimes before I realized that he thought I was being silly and calling him food when I called him "Sugar." That made me laugh too!

The next time we FaceTimed, I asked him, "Do you know why I call you 'Sugar'"? He replied, "No, Hot Dog." I explained that we use sugar to make cakes and cookies and icing because it is sweet. "And while I like cakes and cookies and icing, I love you. So I call you 'Sugar.'" The next time he saw me, he called me "Sugar." Doesn't that just touch your heart? It touched mine. Most of the time, he calls me "Grandma Betz," but intermingled in our together time is "Sugar."

As Christians we need to choose our words carefully to avoid being misunderstood. As we speak, we may need to avoid catch phrases or words that we know the meaning of, but others may not. When Jesus spoke to Nicodemus, a Pharisee—one of Israel's teachers, He had to explain what He meant by being born again (John 3:3–8). Today there are many Christian phrases and sayings that we understand in our Christian circles. But when speaking with someone who has never been to a Bible-believing church, we need to be considerate and take time to use words they can understand. Our message gets lost if the listeners are hearing from a different perspective. We should always ask the Holy Spirit to speak through us and give us discernment when some of our words need an explanation.

Recently I was in a Bible study where the study book asked for our reaction to a verse in the book of Ephesians. One of the ladies said, "It took me forever just to find Ephesians!" This was her first Bible study. None of the leaders thought to acquaint our ladies with a quick overview of how the Bible is laid out, especially mentioning the Table of Contents at the beginning.

I am so grateful that our heavenly Father gave us His Word and sent us the Holy Spirit (John 14:16–17) who teaches us what we need to know.

> *All Scripture is inspired by God and is useful to teach us what is true and to make us realize what is wrong in our lives. It corrects us when we are wrong and teaches us to do what is right. God uses it to prepare and equip his people to do every good work.*
> *—2 Timothy 3:16–17 NLT*

Plan of Action

1. Consider some of the phrases Christians use in our everyday language—words such as *born again, saved, repent, discern*. We may understand these terms, but people who are new Christians or nonbelievers may not understand them. Therefore, we need to use words they can understand too. Even in my neighborhood Bible study after I have explained a word or a Scripture, I ask the group if they understood what I said. Then I wait an appropriate amount of time for them to reply.

2. When someone asks, "What is the Bible?" You can take the person to 2 Timothy 3:16–17: "*All Scripture is God-breathed and is useful for teaching, rebuking, correcting and training in righteousness, so that the servant* [that is us] *of God may be thoroughly equipped for every good work*" (2 Timothy 3:16–17). If the person is new to the Bible, you can take them to that verse in the *New International Version* or *English Standard Version* translation or even a paraphrased Bible such as *The New Living Translation* or *The Message*. Praise God that we have such a variety of Bibles to choose from!

Prayer

Lord, we know that whatever You give us to do, You will help us with it. Please teach us what You want us to know. We want to be literate Christians, and we always need help when we are trying to tell others about You and Your Word. We trust You, Jesus. We pray in Your name. Amen.

PETER

Scripture Reading: Mark 16:1–7

"But go, tell his disciples and Peter, 'He is going ahead of you into Galilee. There you will see him, just as he told you'" (Mark 16:7).

When Mary Magdalene and Mary the mother of the Apostle James, and Salome came to Jesus' tomb to anoint Jesus' body, they were surprised to see that the stone had been rolled away. They entered the tomb and saw *"a young man dressed in a white robe"* (Mark 16:5). This young man told the women that Jesus had risen. Then he gave them a message for *"his [Jesus'] disciples and Peter."*

Why would he have singled out Peter? Wasn't he one of the disciples too? Yes, Peter was one of Christ's disciples. In fact, he was the disciple who said that even if he were threatened with death, he would stand by Christ. But he fell away when reality hit and the soldiers arrested Christ. In fact, he denied even knowing Christ (Luke 22:54–62). Jesus knew that Peter felt great remorse over having denied Him, and He wanted Peter to know that he was forgiven and that He still loved him.

Did you know that atop the Roman Catholic churches in Bavaria is a cross, but a rooster stands atop the Protestant churches? We were told that the Protestant churches have a rooster to remind all who enter that Christ loved and forgave Peter even though after Jesus was arrested, Peter denied knowing Him three times before the rooster crowed. This rooster exemplifies the fact that Christ's love and forgiveness extend to all sinners who repent.

The message behind the symbol is a wonderful encouragement to us sinners. When we read Romans 3:23, we see that all of us are sinners. None of us is a match for God's holiness. But thanks be to God He sent Christ as the sacrifice for our sin, and we are forgiven the minute we repent, just like Peter was.

Plan of Action

1. Years ago, one of our Bible study friends told us something we still remember. When it comes to sin, we need to keep short accounts. In other words, at the moment you know you have sinned, ask for forgiveness. Don't wallow in how you have failed. Just ask Christ for His forgiveness. *"If we confess our sins, he is faithful and just and will forgive us our sins and purify us from all unrighteousness"* (1 John 1:9). Once we confess our sin, our slate is wiped clean. It is as though we never sinned.

2. Are you in a group Bible study? If not, consider looking into one either in your neighborhood or in your church. I recommend finding one in which the group is actually studying the Scripture as opposed to studying some person's ideas. There are many good study books that lead you to look into the Bible deeply.

3. Test the group to see if it is one you want to join. Ask yourself, "How do they treat Jesus?" (He is God, our Savior, who came to the earth as a baby and grew to manhood without sin. Then He died on the cross as the sacrifice for our sins, a sacrifice for all who accept Him, and He arose on the third day. He is alive today and forever. He is the only way to the Father.) If they deny that Jesus is the Son of God, or if they say He was a great prophet but not really God, run away. Find another church.

4. Next you want to find out how they treat the Holy Spirit. (He is part of the Triune God who came from heaven to live in us when we accept Jesus as our Savior and Lord. He reminds us what Jesus taught, and He comforts us when we hurt.) Be sure the emphasis is on the Bible, where you study our Triune God: Father, Son, and Holy Spirit. There is a very popular "church" that does not believe in the Holy Spirit. Of course they don't say that. Instead, they encourage their followers to trust in themselves. They tell them they can do anything if they just believe in themselves. The truth is that I can do anything that God wants me to do. The Holy Spirit who lives in me will help me throughout my life. He can do awesome things with and through me as I trust in Him. It's by His help that I am able to do amazing things.

5. Once you have decided on a Bible study group, do your homework. Then when you go through the discussion, you will hear the Scriptures twice. The more we hear something, the quicker we will learn it.

Prayer

Lord, how I love Your Word! You have made it alive and significant for our everyday lives. Of course, the more we read it, the better we know You. Thank You for Your presence in our lives. Thank You for pointing out things in our lives that don't please You, so we can work with You to change. Thank You that we can confess our sins to You, and You are so loving and gracious to forgive us. I love You, Lord. I pray in Your Son's name. Amen.

THE PROUD FATHER

Scripture Reading: Psalm 139:1–18, 23–24

"As soon as Jesus was baptized, he went up out of the water. At that moment heaven was opened, and he saw the Spirit of God descending like a dove and lighting on him. And a voice from heaven said, 'This is my Son, whom I love; with him I am well pleased' "
(Matthew 3:16–17).

It occurred to me the other day that I don't think I have ever thought of our heavenly Father in His role as the Father of Christ our Savior. You are probably asking, "What do you mean, and how can that be? After all, we know God is our heavenly Father, and we know that Jesus is His Son." True. But this time, I am considering the fact that our Father was proud of Jesus.

When I read Matthew 3:16–17, quoted above, and when I read Luke 3:21–22, which is Luke's description of the same event, I found a new perspective. "When all the people were being baptized, Jesus was baptized too. And as he was praying, heaven was opened and the Holy Spirit descended on him in bodily form like a dove.

And a voice came from heaven: 'You are my Son, whom I love; with you I am well pleased.'" Before Jesus came to the earth, He was in heaven with the Father and the Holy Spirit. When Jesus came to the earth, He was separated from the Father. So how wonderful it must have been for Christ to hear His Father speak to Him so all could hear! I believe these Scriptures show that as God looked at the first thirty years of Christ's sinless life, He let everyone know that He was so very proud of His Son. And then the Holy Spirit descended on Him. What a blessing for them and for those who witnessed the event. They were eyewitnesses of our Triune God.

Once in a while, I hear of parents who withhold praises from their children for fear they might become spoiled. The Scripture quoted above shows that praising our children when they do something well will not spoil them. However, we do realize that Christ was perfect and sinless, unlike both our children and us (Romans 3:23). Nevertheless, I believe that when our children do something praiseworthy, we should follow God's example and praise them.

Now let's bring this closer to home. Do you ever feel that the Father is pleased with you? If not, my heart breaks for you. Let's go to Scripture once again.

First, have you accepted Jesus as your Savior? Jesus speaks of Himself in John 3:16: "*For God so loved the world that he gave his one and only Son, that whoever believes in him shall not perish but have eternal life.*" Then in Romans 10:9 the Apostle Paul tells us: "*If you confess with your mouth, 'Jesus is Lord,' and believe in your heart that God raised him from the dead, you will be saved.*" If you have not yet accepted Christ's death on your behalf, as the sacrifice for your sins, ask God to lift the veil of unbelief that you have. Ask Him to give you the faith to believe.

If you have accepted Christ's sacrifice for your life, I give you John 1:12: "*To all who received him, to those who believed in his name, he gave the right to become children of God.*" You are God's child, and you can accept His many promises in His Word. For example, in Deuteronomy 31:6, He promises us that He'll never leave us or forsake us. Paul, inspired by the Holy Spirit, encourages us in Colossians 3:12a: "*Therefore as God's chosen people, holy and dearly loved.*" Please read one of my favorite chapters in the Bible: Psalm 139:1–18, 23–24. The last Scripture that I want to draw your attention to is Psalm 138:8a: "*The Lord will fulfill his purpose for me; your love, O Lord, endures forever.*" Yes, Lord, You will fulfill Your purpose for us, and Your love endures forever.

Now that we have established that God is not only pleased with you but in fact, He loves you, let's look at examples of times when He has been pleased with you. Have you ever felt God's nudge to step out of your comfort zone and do a work for Him? Have you felt God was leading you to do some very good action? Then you did it and knew that was God's nudge. Do you remember how good you felt, even affirmed? God is always pleased with obedience. In fact, in the Old Testament Samuel states that God prefers obedience to sacrifices (1 Samuel 15:22b). In John 14:21 Jesus informs us "*Whoever has my commands and obeys them, he is the one who loves me. He who loves me will be loved by my Father, and I too will love him and show myself to him*" Our Father loves you, and Jesus loves you. Furthermore, as His child, you are His "*treasured possession*" (Exodus 19:5).

Did you know that even before you became a Christian and before you started your journey of following His lead, God loved you? Let's look at Romans 5:8. "*But God demonstrates his own love for us in this: While we were still sinners, Christ died for us.*" He has known us all our lives, and He knows the very worst things we have done. Yet He loves us, and Christ even died for us despite our ugliness. But lovingly, kindly, graciously the Holy Spirit works in us, cleaning us, changing us to become more like Christ.

Tasha Layton sings a song entitled "Look What You've Done." In it she recalls how her life was spiraling down until God picked her up and changed her. I have a similar feeling when I read God's gift to me—my writing. Please understand that I am not patting myself on the back. I know fully that I only have this gift because He works through me. He gives me the idea, and then He gives me the words. I am in awe of Him, and say in reverence, "Oh, Lord, look what You have done. Thank You so much! It is so much better than my writing would be on my own."

Do you know what your spiritual gift is? You may even have several gifts. If you don't know what spiritual gift you have, ask God to enlighten you. Then ask your pastor if he has a "test" you could take to identify your gift(s). Meanwhile you can go to www.gotquestions.com to see a listing of some of the gifts attached with the Scripture references.

Once we know our gifts, we are to use them for the glory of God (Colossians 3:17) and to serve in our church *"for the common good"* (1 Corinthians 12:4–7). Paul told Timothy to *"fan into flame the gift of God"* (2 Timothy 1:6). In other words, we are to put our gifts to work for the building up of our church. Many times, God calls us to use our gifts in our neighborhoods or other places we are involved. When I use my gifts, I know God is pleased with me. In addition, there are times when I see that someone needs help, and although the deed is out of my gift realm, I know He is asking me to step in and help. My point is this: yes, we should use our gifts—absolutely—but we should also be ready to serve however He calls us to. The key here is however He calls us.

Plan of Action

1. For those of you who have not yet recognized the fact that Christ died for you, please write down the date today. Mark it as the specific time that you are asking God to make His presence obvious in your life. Then please open your eyes to see what God will do.

2. For those of you who have already accepted Christ's sacrifice on your behalf, I want you to take some time looking for those moments when you have followed God's nudge. Make note of them in a journal. Record the date if you remember, and record your feelings at the time. What was God asking you to do? How are you sure that it was God's nudge? What was the result of your following God's direction? If you remember several nudges, write those down too. These will serve as reminders of God's love for you when you are feeling low.

Prayer

Oh, my Lord, draw us ever closer to You. Help us as we grow up in You. Thank You for Your love. Thank You that You love us enough to lead and teach us. Thank You for Your call on our lives. Father, if there is a reader who doesn't yet know that You love him or her, please make Your love visible in his or her life. I ask that all we do please You and glorify You. Thank You, Father. In Jesus' name I pray. Amen.

REFLECTION

Scripture Reading: Ephesians 3:14–19

"For God so loved the world, that he gave his only Son, that whoever believes in him should not perish but have eternal life" (John 3:16 ESV).

"How great is the love the Father has lavished on us, that we should be called children of God! And that is what we are" (1 John 3:1)!

A friend sent me a link to watch our church's Sunday evening praise service. As I watched, I found that I could either concentrate on my church family praising my Lord, or I could inspect my reflection which was also visible on my phone. Of course, that is no surprise to those of you who have smart phones. Most of us have taken "selfies."

This exercise made me consider how much time we spend reflecting on ourselves compared with the amount of time we reflect on others. As Christians we should have a good balance of self-reflection in the light of God's word, worshiping, and serving others all to His glory.

I must admit that when I look at my reflection, I tend to be critical. Rather than reacting as I should—thanking God that He chose to create me and draw me into His family—I see my wrinkles, the extra pounds I need to lose, and so one. A while ago one of my pastors said, "As a child of God's covenant, you are called to love all that your God loves, and your God loves you." Of course, we know this in our heads since throughout His word He continually expresses His love for us. It is magnified in John 3:16 quoted above.

No matter how the world sees us and no matter how we see ourselves, God Almighty, creator of all that is, loves us and wants us to know that not only does He love us, but He also created us for His special purposes. First Thessalonians 1:4 explains that *"God not only loves you very much but also has put His hand on you for something special"* (MSG). He is with us always and will be with us always as Deuteronomy 31:8 promises, *"The* LORD *himself goes before you and will be with you; he will never leave you nor forsake you. Do not be afraid; do not be discouraged."*

Amazingly, God loved us even before we were born, even before we knew of Him (Psalm 139:13). Then Psalm 139:14 reminds us that we are *"wonderfully made; your works are wonderful."* We are His works, and we are wonderful because He says so—even with wrinkles and a few extra pounds.

Plan of Action

1. Since we tend to be critical of ourselves, let's look around and see if there is someone who could use a verbal boost. I used to teach grades 7–12. Most kids of that age tend to be overly critical of themselves. Thus, today when I see kids who fall in that age group, I try to find a reason to compliment them. Since I don't want to embarrass them, I wait until they are

without their peers, or I say it very quietly. When you do this, they blossom right in front of you. Or maybe they won't. But I am sure they will remember what you said.

2. From now on when we see a reflection of ourselves, let's try to thank God for His love and for the fact that He loved us before we were born. He loves us now. And He will love us forever; His love never ceases. Lamentations 3:22–23 is such a blessing: *"The steadfast love of the LORD never ceases; his mercies never come to an end; they are new every morning; great is your faithfulness* (ESV).

Prayer

Father, forgive me for being so critical of Your work—me. You knit me together in my mother's womb, and I am fearfully and wonderfully made. Please help me to do everything to Your glory and honor and in Your love. Let me be a blessing to You and to those You place in my path. Help me to walk with You every minute of every day. Open my eyes to see people who need a boost, some encouragement. Thank You for Your love. I love You, Lord, and I pray in Jesus' name. Amen.

RESIST THE DEVIL

Scripture Reading: Exodus 20:1–17

"Submit yourselves, then, to God. Resist the devil, and he will flee from you." (James 4:7).

When I was in my twenties and had been married for five years, I carpooled with a fellow teacher for our forty-five-minute drive to school. We had known each other for a few months, and he knew I was a Christian.

One day, he asked, "What if God told you to have an affair?" I answered without skipping a beat, "God wouldn't ask me to do that because it is against His law, the Bible." He countered with, "Well, just consider it. What would you do if He told you to have an affair?" Again, I answered, "He wouldn't tell me to do that because it is against His law."

Today my husband and I have been married for fifty-five years. When I look back on that conversation, I see it even more clearly now. He wanted to plant a seed of unfaithfulness, hoping I would consider it . . . think about it. But I didn't. God was faithful to make me not even reflect on it, and to let this fellow teacher know in no uncertain terms that it wasn't open for discussion. Praise God for that. The Holy Spirit made me strong and unmovable. I also stopped carpooling with him.

Satan uses humans to try to plant thought-seeds of evil. He tries to make it seem as if it is not all that bad to think of or consider doing a sinful act. In Matthew 5:27–28, Jesus said, *"You have heard it said, 'Do not commit adultery.' But I tell you that anyone who looks at a woman lustfully has already committed adultery with her in his heart."* Psalm 101:3a states: *"I will set before my eyes no vile thing."* Then we read Psalm101:4b: *"I will have nothing to do with evil."*

Years ago, I did one of Beth Moore's Bible studies. Each week we began by watching her teach on a video. She said something that has stayed with me; she said we need to guard our eyes because that is where sin can begin. You see someone attractive and begin to consider what life would be like with him or her. The view enters your brain where you begin to entertain unhealthy, unfaithful thoughts, and off your mind goes. Or maybe you see your neighbor's car, and you begin to think how nice it would be to have that car, or his wife, or his job. You get the picture. Guard your eyes.

My friends laugh at me because I have adopted an attitude of gratitude. When there is a handsome gentleman at our community pool, I literally thank God for creating this fine looking fellow. Right away my mind goes to our Lord, and I admire His work . . . briefly.

I want to take a moment to encourage anyone who has been tempted and still feels guilty about it. In my first book, *Lord, It's Time for Just You and Me,* I wrote about an incident that happened to me around the same time as the incident with the carpooling coworker. One afternoon, I was standing in the school hallway visiting with another teacher after classes were finished for the day, when one of my tall, male students walked over to me, placed his hand over my head, and grinned as he leaned uncomfortably close, ostensibly to ask about an assignment. As quickly as he took a position of power, towering over my five-foot-three frame, I felt my face flush. For a mere flash of a moment, I knew temptation. Praise God, He gave me the sense to step out from under this boy's arm and assume my teacher role, gaining control of the situation. I told him he needed to get back to track practice.

Nevertheless, I was angry and so disappointed with myself for being tempted. I was a solid, growing, actively-seeking-God's-way-in-my-life Christian. I couldn't believe I was tempted, if even for a flash of a minute. I agonized over this until the Lord graciously reminded me that even Jesus was tempted (Matthew 4:1–10). Jesus was perfect, yet He was still tempted. The experience of being tempted is not a sin. We sin only if we act on that temptation: if we accept the invitation and take the next step. The Lord didn't say we wouldn't be tempted; He said He would give us a way to escape a temptation (1 Corinthians 10:13). Thank You, Lord!

I write this in case you have been tempted, and you continue to feel guilty because of that. Don't take that guilt! If you fled from that temptation, you are not guilty. Remember Satan loves to accuse us and make us feel guilty (Revelation 12:10), whether there is a reason or not. When we do sin, we confess it immediately. We do not wallow and say to ourselves, "Oh my. I am a sinner. I can't do anything right. Blah, blah, blah." Nope! You confess your sin immediately when you recognize you have sinned; you accept God's forgiveness; and move on in your life with a clean slate.

Plan of Action

1. Ask the Lord if there are any unhealthy thoughts lingering in your mind that He needs to cleanse. Wait on Him. When something comes to your mind, lay it before God. Ask Him to forgive you, and leave it with Him.

2. Forgive yourself for entertaining unhealthy thoughts. Now move on. If and when those memories come back, reject them in Jesus' name. Purposely busy your mind with something else—say an appropriate Scripture, think of several Scriptures, or play Christian music if you can.

3. One of my pastors instructed us that if someone brings up our sinful behavior from our past, respond with, "No, that _____ (write your name here) no longer exists. I became a new creation when I accepted Christ" (2 Corinthians 5:17). You might humbly add that you have confessed that sin, and you have been forgiven. You have a clean slate.

Prayer

Lord, we know that You gave us the Ten Commandments to delineate the type of behavior and thoughts we should have as Your children. In addition to those, You have given us information throughout Your Word illustrating the appropriate behavior for Your followers. Lord, You also know that we are prone to sin because of our human nature. Therefore, we need Your strength to help us to refuse temptations and maintain our sinless walk with You. God, we need You. We desperately need Your help. We love You so much and want to walk faithfully with You. We trust that You will help us, Lord. We pray in the name of Jesus, our precious Savior. Amen.

THE RICH MAN

Scripture Reading: Mark 10:17–31

"What must I do to inherit eternal life" (Mark 10:17)?

Many, many times I have heard the story of the rich man who asked Jesus, *"What must I do to inherit eternal life?"* However, today was the first time that verse 21 of Mark 10 stood out to me. *"Jesus looked at him and loved him."* When I read the story previously, I pictured Jesus looking down with disdain on this rich man. But no. The Scripture says, *"Jesus looked at him and loved him"* (Mark 10:21a). I am sure you remember the rest of the story, which is in Mark 10:17–31. The rich man went away sad because Jesus told him that although he had kept the commandments, he needed to do one more thing: *"Go, sell everything you have and give it to the poor, and you will have treasure in heaven. Then come, follow me"* (Mark 10:21).

We know that God is not opposed to the rich or to riches. What is crucial is that we are not to worship wealth. God will not allow money, possessions, or people to take His place as number one in our lives. He is preeminent. We are to have one God, and that is God almighty, Creator of heaven and earth (Colossians 1:16). The rich man felt that his money was more important than giving all he had to the poor and following Jesus. When Jesus saw him, He already knew he had kept all the commandments. Jesus also knew that his riches took priority over God. The rich man loved his riches more than he loved Jesus.

Now I am going out on a limb here. What I am about to say is not listed in the Scriptures. I just know how graciously God works with me. When I ask Him to point out anything in me that makes Him sad, He usually only points to one of my imperfections at a time. When He makes me aware of an imperfection, He gives me time for us to work that out of my character. I hope that Christ did the same for the rich man. Of course, we don't know if he loosened his grip on his riches since that is not the main message of this story. But that is my hope.

Plan of Action

1. Ask yourself if you have placed anything above God as your god. Think over your life. We are to love God above everyone and everything else in our lives. If you aren't sure, ask God to show you. If you know you have someone or something that is holding the place that only belongs to God, ask Him to help you loosen your hold. I love Philippians 2:13 *"For it is God who works in you to will and to act according to his good purpose."* If you are at least willing for God to change you, He will.

2. Join me in praying for our family, friends, neighbors, business colleagues, and even you and me. Let's pray that we look to God to reveal how we are to bless others with our wealth, whether it is a wealth of knowledge, experience, or financial assets. One reason God gives us an abundance of something

is so He can bless others through us. Many years ago, one of my friends told me that God doesn't usually do a one-way blessing; He blesses the giver as well as the recipient. Thank You, God!

Prayer

Lord, please help us to never put anything above You. If we are giving priority to anyone or anything, please point that out, and help us to open our hands, and give it to You. I am in awe of the fact that You love us and want to help us. Your Word tells us that You go before us and will be with us, that You will never leave us or forsake us (Deuteronomy 31:8). This tells us that You are aware of our every move. Please help us to bless You in everything we do. We pray in the name of our beautiful Creator, Jesus. Amen.

SCATTERING SEED

Scripture Reading: Matthew 13:1–23

"This is what the kingdom of God is like. A man scatters seed on the ground. Night and day, whether he sleeps or gets up, the seed sprouts and grows, though he does not know how. All by itself the soil produces grain—first the stalk, then the head, then the full kernel in the head. As soon as the grain is ripe, he puts the sickle to it, because the harvest has come" (Mark 4:26–29).

We "scatter seed" as we go through life by speaking and living our faith. The results are not up to us beyond our being faithful to speak His Word and follow Him. He produces the results and harvest.

This is great comfort to me when I look at some of my very dear friends and see no results of the seed I've scattered in their lives. I question my effectiveness as one of His ambassadors, one of His teachers, one of His servants. But just when I am discouraged because I see no growth in the seed I've scattered, He leads me to a passage in His Word like Mark 4:26–29 and reminds that He is responsible for the spiritual growth in every person. I am not.

I am responsible to follow Him obediently and to pray that He will lift their veils of unbelief (2 Corinthians 3:14) as He draws them to Him.

We serve a great God *"who is able to do immeasurably more than we can ask or imagine"* (Ephesians 3:20)!

Plan of Action

1. As you look at some of the seeds you have scattered, pray that they have fallen on good soil.

2. Ask God to lift the veils of unbelief from those who are in your circle of friends, relatives, even strangers that God has placed in your path.

3. Remember that once the seed is scattered, it is up to God to produce the harvest of faith in Christ.

Prayer

Lord, please prepare me to hear Your voice and follow Your guidance as I speak Your words in season and out of season as Your Word says in 2 Timothy 4:2. I know that I am to correct, rebuke, and encourage—with great patience and careful instruction. Only with You, Lord, is this possible. Thank You for Your patient instruction, and thank You for lifting the veil of unbelief from those to whom I speak on Your behalf. I pray in Jesus' name. Amen.

SEIZE THE IDEA!

Scripture Reading: Psalm 32:8–11 and 1 Samuel 3:1–10

"I will praise the LORD, who counsels me; even at night my heart instructs me" (Psalm 16:7).

Have you ever awakened in the night and had a great idea that you were sure you would remember in the morning? Me too. At the time, I felt too sleepy to get up and write down the idea. Then when I awoke in the morning, that great idea He gave me in the middle of the night was lost. I couldn't remember it. Now, whenever He gives me an idea, even if I am involved with some activity, I write down the crux of the idea right away.

Today, when I was in the middle of pool aerobics, He gave me something that needed to put into the "Suggestions for Using This Devotional" section of this book. Since there was neither pen nor paper close, I scooted over to two of the ladies exercising next to me, and I asked them to remind me about the Bible when we finished exercising. They remembered to remind me, and I got out of the pool and wrote down the idea with the pen and paper in my beach bag. Another day, He gave me an entirely new idea for a devotional while I was doing pool aerobics, and since I was the leader that day, I could take a minute and write down the crux of the idea in the "Reminders" part of my phone.

He continues to instruct me in so many ways, as I am sure He does you too. Don't you love when He gives you new ideas? *"Call to me and I will answer you and tell you great and unsearchable things you do not know"* (Jeremiah 33:3). Yes, Lord, please tell us great and unsearchable things we do not know. We want to allow Him to teach us perpetually until we see Him face to face (1 Corinthians 13:12). We also want to have ears to hear (Matthew 11:15) anytime He wants to tell us something.

Plan of Action

1. Are you trying to make a decision, but you are not sure which you should choose, or which way to go? Ask God to give you ears to hear His instruction. Then listen. He may answer you right away. With me He answers when I am in the middle of doing other things or when I am having my quiet time and reading the Bible. Just be sure you stay aware and listen.

2. Over and over in the Bible we are told that if we ask our Lord for direction, He will answer us. Matthew 7:7–8 tells us:

   Ask and it will be given to you; seek and you will find; knock and the door will be opened to you. For everyone who asks receives; the one who seeks finds; and to the one who knocks, the door will be opened.

When He gives you an idea, write it down, and put the date on it. How fun to look back and see how and when He speaks to you!

Prayer

My Lord and my God, how generous You are with us! Father, please teach us to hear You when You speak to us. Please teach us to be still and listen for Your voice. You say that your sheep can tell the difference between Your voice and others. Help us to trust the Holy Spirit to direct us and give us discernment. We know we are a privileged people because You love us and have called us to follow You. We love You, our precious Lord, and we pray in Jesus' name. Amen.

THE SON IS INVADING MY SHADE

Scripture Reading: Hebrews 12:1–11

"Search me, O God, and know my heart! Try me and know my thoughts! And see if there be any wicked way in me, and lead me in the way everlasting"
(Psalm 139:23–24 RSV)!

I was sitting in the shade at the swimming pool on a particularly hot Florida day. My two friends and I had finished pool aerobics in the previous hour, and we were doing what we considered a bonus to our exercise. We were chatting. As time moved on, so did the invasion of the sun peeking around the umbrella pushing out my shade, which was making me uncomfortably warm.

This made me think of the way the Lord, the Son of God, deals with me when there is something in me that needs to be changed. Just when I think I am pretty good in His eyes and have rid myself of all my bad habits, He shines His light on another area of my life that needs to change. He invades my comfort and steps on my pride. I am bummed to find out there is another part of me that is not yet as He wants. Nevertheless, I am grateful that usually He only deals with eradicating my "shaded" habits one at a time.

I refer to this as His using His Holy Spirit SOS scrubbing pad on my "shady" areas. It's not fun, but it's necessary. Ken Taylor paraphrased Psalm 139:24 this way: *"Point out anything you find in me that makes you sad, and lead me along the path of everlasting life"* (TLB). I truly want Him to do that. I don't want to make my Lord sad. Ephesians 4:22–24 tells us:

> *You were taught with regard to your former way of life, to put off your old self, which is corrupted by its deceitful desires; to be made new in the attitude of your minds; and to put on the new self, created to be like God in true righteousness and holiness.*

We serve such a gracious God that He never tells us to do something that He expects us to do on our own. He loves us, and He wants to help us. We see that in Philippians 2:13: *"For it is God who works in you to will and to act according to his good purpose."* He works in us to help us do what He wants. *"The Lord will fulfill his purpose for me; your love, O Lord, endures forever—do not abandon the works of your hands"* (Psalm 138:8). Yes, please, Lord, do not abandon the works of your hands.

Plan of Action

1. It's time to ask Him to point out anything in us that makes Him sad. Just as You spoke light into the darkness in Genesis 1:3, Lord, please shine Your light on our shady areas. We want to *"live a life worthy of the calling* [we] *have received"* (Ephesians 4:1b); that can only be done with Your help.

2. As much as we would like to think we have our lives very well put together, we will not be perfect until we see Christ face to face. Therefore, we need to be open for Him to work with us

and making us to be more like Christ. His shining light may come in many different ways; He may speak through a pastor, a friend, in a Bible study, or even in our own private devotion time. Remember that if we are not dead, He's not done with us. He loves us and won't ever leave us alone (Deuteronomy 31:6; Joshua 1:5; 1 Chronicles 28:20).

Prayer

Father, You know that I truly want You to wash me with Your Word. Please sharpen my senses so that I hear You clearly. Then, Lord, please help me to obey Your directions. I love Philippians 2:13 where You tell us that You will help us do Your will. What a wonderful God You are! Thank You for loving us. Thank You for taking care of us. Thank You for giving us Your Word. Thank You for giving us Jesus! It is in His name I pray. Amen.

THE STONE HAD BEEN ROLLED AWAY

Scripture Reading: Matthew 28:1–10

"On the evening of that first day of the week, when the disciples were together, with the doors locked for fear of the Jewish leaders, Jesus came and stood among them and said, 'Peace be with you'" (John 20:19)!

"A week later his disciples were in the house again, and Thomas was with them. Though the doors were locked, Jesus came and stood among them and said, 'Peace be with you'" (John 20:26)!

One of the puzzles for the people in Jesus' time was who rolled the stone away from the entrance to Jesus' tomb. Matthew 28:2 states that an angel of the Lord rolled it back and sat on it. Consider this: Jesus didn't need the stone to be rolled away in order to be raised, brought back to life, on the third day. Read the two quoted Scriptures above. He appeared to his disciples without going through the door. The door was locked. The stone was rolled away from the opening to the tomb for our benefit and to prove to the world that He had indeed risen just as He and the prophets had foretold.

Consider this: Jesus is the Creator of the entire world. He created the stone that was placed in front of the tomb where He was buried. Of course, we know from reading Matthew 27:62–66 that after Jesus' dead body had been placed in the tomb, the chief priests and Pharisees asked Pilate to secure the tomb. Since Jesus had said that after three days He would rise again (Matthew 16:21), they wanted to be sure that none of His disciples would come and steal His body and claim that He had arisen. Pilate told them to place a guard at the tomb, and they secured the tomb with a seal on the stone.

The stone that Christ had created could no more hold His body in the tomb than I could move the Eiffel Tower. Do you remember when Jesus was riding the colt going down the Mount of Olives and His disciples were praising God? (Luke 19:28–40) Some of the Pharisees told Jesus to rebuke His disciples, and Jesus said, *"I tell you if they keep quiet, the stones will cry out"* (Luke 19:40). I wonder if the stone that covered the tomb praised Jesus while guarding Him.

Plan of Action

1. Let's ask God to open our hearts and minds to see all He wants of us and for us. He is not limited by a lack of anything. He owns it all. Let's see His vision for us and then rely on Him to help us fulfill that vision.

2. Keeping in mind that this earth belongs to Him, let's do our best to take good care of it. Usually, when I think of being a good steward, I think of taking care of the finances He gives us. But I believe we are also supposed to take good care of all that He has given us: our families, our homes, our neighbors, our land, the earth.

Prayer

Lord, teach me to truly be a good steward of all You have given me. Teach me to open my heart and mind to see all that You want for me, this day and in the future. Train me not to limit myself with my own vision. You are immeasurably greater than all I can think or imagine. Please use me whenever and wherever You wish. I love You, my Lord and my Savior, my God and my Father, and my Holy Spirit and Teacher. I pray in the powerful name of Jesus. Amen.

THE STORM

Scripture Reading: Mark 4:35–41

"Jesus was in the stern, sleeping on a cushion. The disciples woke him and said to him, 'Teacher, don't you care if we drown'" (Mark 4:38)?

It is important to remember as we read the "Scripture Reading" above that this storm was big enough that it frightened even the seasoned fishermen.

I never thought of this before, but Satan was allowed to amp up the storm and probably thought he would drown both Christ and His disciples. However, the disciples awakened Jesus, who was asleep on the boat, and He then quieted the wind and the waves. To this the disciples *"were terrified and asked each other, 'Who is this? Even the wind and the waves obey him'"* (Mark 4:41)!

We know there was another time when the disciples were in a boat which was threatened by the wind and the waves. This is recorded in Matthew 14:22–32 when Jesus stayed on land to be alone and pray. He sent the disciples ahead in their boat. This is the episode where Peter realizes that Christ is walking on the water by their boat, and he asks Christ to invite him to walk to

Him on the water. Peter was successful until he saw the wind and became afraid. Of course, Jesus saved him from drowning. As they both climbed into the boat, the disciples *"worshiped him, saying, 'Truly you are the Son of God'"* (Matthew 14:33).

Have you ever been in a storm and felt sure that your life was in danger? I grew up in Kansas where I experienced some humdingers. Many times, my family and I went to our basement, huddled under my father's solid walnut desk while covering ourselves with comforters to protect us from possible flying debris from a tornado. I have seen tall trees bend to a right angle but still not break.

In my first book, *Lord, It's Time for Just You and Me,* under the title "Fear and Faith" (page 88), I described the time when our four-year-old daughter and I were reading a book just before bedtime. Suddenly, the gentle rain changed into a frightening sound when a huge wind began to smash the rain against our window. Our daughter reminded me that Jesus told the wind to stop in the Bible, and so she spoke out loud, "Storm, stop in Jesus' name!" At that moment the storm's fury stopped. The harsh wind stopped. Our Lord lovingly and graciously calmed the storm in an answer to a young girl's step in faith.

Perhaps you are in a figurative storm rather than a weather storm, and you, like the disciples, are afraid you are going to sink. Reach out your hand to Jesus. He is able to keep you afloat. If you think that you are too bad or insignificant for Jesus to save you, you are wrong. *"But God demonstrates his own love for us in this: While we were still sinners, Christ died for us"* (Romans 5:8). None of us is worthy of His attention, let alone His lifting us out of a bad situation. The truth is He loves us. He knows the worst about us, and He still loves us and wants to save us. He doesn't wait until we have our whole world in order before He reaches down to help us. He died for us *"while we were sinners."* Call out to Him, and ask Him to calm the storm. He is able. *"In you, LORD, I have taken refuge; let me never be put to shame. In your righteousness, rescue me and deliver me; turn your ear to me and save me"* (Psalm 71:1–2).

Plan of Action

1. Satan does his best to mess with us, to scare us. But remember Jesus conquered death and the evil one. *"You, dear children, are from God and . . . the one* [the Holy Spirit] *who is in you is greater than the one* [Satan] *who is in the world"* (1 John 4:4).

2. Our God promises in His Word to watch over us. Ask God to help you memorize some Scriptures to remind you that He protects you. Here are two of my favorites that I have memorized:

   "Though I walk in the midst of trouble, you preserve my life. You stretch out your hand against the anger of my foes; with your right hand you save me" (Psalm 138:7).

   "Yes, though a mighty army marches against me, my heart shall know no fear! I am confident that God will save me" (Psalm 27:3 TLB).

If you are considering suicide, don't fight this battle alone. Please call 988 if you are in the U.S. You can also call 1-800-273-TALK (800-273-8255).

I also want you to contact your pastor. If you don't have one, I recommend that you find one of the largest churches in your area because large churches usually have several pastors who cover different needs within the church. Call the church and ask for the pastor who could help you.

Prayer

Father, You know about my storms. Please calm them. I thank You that I can speak to them in Jesus' name and command them to calm down. Give me wisdom as to how to react when a storm appears, whether it is a threatening weather storm or a storm in the circumstances in my life. Please, my loving and faithful Father, protect me and remind me that I don't have to be afraid. As Your child, I am truly loved and blessed. Thank You, Lord. In Jesus' name I pray. Amen.

THORNS AND THISTLES

Scripture Reading: Hebrews 5:11–6:8

"Land that drinks in the rain often falling on it and that produces a crop useful to those for whom it is farmed receives the blessing of God. But land that produces thorns and thistles is worthless and is in danger of being cursed. In the end it will be burned" (Hebrews 6:7–8).

As followers of Christ, we are like the land that drinks in the rain spoken of in Hebrews 6 verse 7. We receive God's blessed teachings. We absorb His Word, and because of His generosity, we produce fruit that is evidenced in our actions and reactions (Galatians 5:22–23). Sadly, there are people who hear God's Word but don't believe it and want nothing to do with it or with God. Those people are like the land that produces thorns and thistles. It is possible that eventually the truth will sink in, and some of them will receive Him. Without Christ they are in danger of being cursed; in the end, they will be burned. This is a serious warning. And yet there are people who ignore it for whatever reason.

There are some other places in the Bible where thorns and thistles are mentioned. In Genesis 3 after Adam and Eve sinned in the garden of Eden, God told Adam that he would have to work the ground from which he would eat *"through painful toil"* (Genesis 3:17). Then God tells him that the ground *"will produce thorns and thistles for you"* (Genesis 3:18). Sometimes, we forget that because of Adam and Eve's sin, death came into the world not only for humans but also for all living things: fruits, vegetables, flowers, trees, animals, and all of creation. There will be no death in heaven. Hallelujah!

Now let's get personal. All of us are producing crops in our speech and our behavior. What kind of crops are we producing: Are they crops that are useful to others or are they full of thorns and thistles? Do we speak life? Or do we speak death? Are most of our thoughts critical and negative, or encouraging and positive? If we are critical and negative in our thoughts, we exhibit that negativity regardless of what our words say. People read attitudes as much as they hear words.

Do people seem to enjoy being around us, or do they avoid us? What kind of people do we attract? Do we tend to attract gossipers? When I was young, my mother told me to be careful around people who gossip. She said, "If they are talking about others to you, they will talk about you to others, and what you say will probably be repeated with your name attached." We read in Proverbs 16:28: *"A perverse person stirs up conflict, and a gossip separates close friends."* Then Proverbs 18:8 tells us: *"The words of a gossip are like choice morsels; they go down the inmost parts."* When we hear gossip, whether it is true or not, it is hard to forget. We wonder if it is true. Gossip can malign a person's character even if it is false. It places a question in our minds about that person. Thankfully, as we mature, we learn to consider the source of the gossip. We learn to avoid some people, but when we can't avoid them, we can choose to disregard their "*morsels.*"

Is it possible that we have developed the habit of being negative or feeling superior to others? Like all habits, this one can be broken. We will have to retrain our thinking. When criticizing another person, pride settles in, and it is pride with no basis. With this in mind, let's look at what the Bible says about our attitude toward ourselves. Romans 12:3 states that we are not to think of ourselves more highly than we ought. Second Samuel 22:28 reads: "*You* [God] *will save the humble people; but Your eyes are on the haughty, that You may bring them down*" (NKJV). Philippians 2:3–4 lists two more of many Scriptures that direct us concerning thoughts ourselves: "*Let nothing be done through selfish ambition or conceit, but in lowliness of mind let each esteem others better than himself. Let each of you look out not only for his own interests, but also for the interests of others*" (NKJV).

We can retrain our thinking by regularly speaking encouragement to ourselves and others. Although at first, we might feel like a hypocrite, after a time, our mind will begin to absorb and believe what we are saying. If our first thought is negative, dismiss it. Over time, our positive speaking will literally change our mind by God's grace.

Let me make a distinction between a knee-jerk negative response and discernment. We are blessed with discernment because the Holy Spirit lives in us and helps us discern truth from lies. Sometimes, He gives us information that is for us alone to protect us from being duped. Sometimes, it is information that could harm others, and it needs to be reported to someone in authority. Of course you will do this after serious prayer, and this is only spoken with someone in authority; it is not discussed with others. The latter would be gossip, and as much as we believe someone is in error, we must leave it with the person in authority to handle. This is as much for our protection as that of others. Just suppose we are wrong. How heartbreaking for us, our friends, and the other person if we spoke our concern to them, and we were wrong.

Plan of Action

1. Take a few moments to look over your last week. Have you been an encourager, or have you been critical most of the time? If you have been critical, decide today that you are changing. I recommend a book by Norman Vincent Peale called *The Power of Positive Thinking*. He also wrote *The Amazing Results of Positive Thinking* and *Enthusiasm Makes a Difference*. He is not just a proponent for positive thinking. He encourages you to lean on God, to call on Him to help you to change your thinking, and to memorize Scripture.

2. If you are not in a Bible-teaching Bible study, find one, and commit to attending. Do your homework and participate. God's word blesses us and washes us.

3. If you are not in a Bible-preaching church, find one, and commit to attend regularly.

Prayer

Father, please help us to dispose of the thorns and thistles in our speech, in our behavior, and in our thoughts. Cleanse us from all thorns and thistles. When we see people who exhibit thorns and thistles, remind us to pray for them. You are such a wonderful loving God. We want to represent You well. Please help us to do that. Thank You, dear, precious, Lord. In Jesus' name we pray. Amen.

A TIME TO WAIT

Scripture Reading: Joshua 2

"After a long time, in the third year, the word of the LORD came to Elijah" (1 Kings 18:1).

Did you read 1 Kings 18:1 quoted above? Elijah waited for God to answer, and He finally did in the third year! Forty-five years ago, I began having a chronic cough. I sought help from more doctors than I can name. I asked the elders at my church to pray for me. But still I continued to cough. It got so bad that I would cough every half hour. Sometimes, I would cough and cough and cough. Most of the time, I would have to leave a meeting and go to a different room until I stopped. Rarely was I able to stay in a church worship service without having to go to a restroom to cough. Yes, I had a period of waiting before the necessary study was done and different medicines tested. But now I can stay through most worship services and meetings. I certainly appreciate the gaps I have between coughing spells. In fact, the other day in pool aerobics, I coughed, and one of my friends said, "You hardly ever cough now! That is great!" Yes, it is! Thank You, Lord.

During this struggle, I so related to the woman in the Bible who had been bleeding for twelve years (Luke 8:40–48). I continued to ask the Lord to heal me, but He didn't for forty-four years. In the forty-fifth year, I went to a wonderful ENT (Ears, Nose and Throat) doctor who knew the right questions to ask and directed me to another doctor who knew about a recent study on those of us who have chronic coughs. He applied the methods he had learned, and I no longer cough every thirty minutes. I still cough sometimes, but nothing like I used to. I have no doubt that God used those doctors to reduce my cough. All praise to Him.

Do you remember Romans 8:28? *"And we know that in all things God works for the good of those who love him, who have been called according to his purpose."* If I hadn't had the cough, I would have continued working outside the home. I have my MBA, and I have been a public school teacher as well as the business manager for my husband's medical practice. However, as my cough began to worsen over the years, I had trouble even answering the phone. God had a different job for me to do. He wanted me to write *Lord, It's Time for Just You and Me.* I felt that I wouldn't be serving Him well by sitting around watching TV. Furthermore, He had told me to write my own devotional when I found none that I liked in a large Christian bookstore. I had lots of time to do that because of the cough, which prohibited me from working in a job outside of our home.

Several years ago, one of the pastors in our church said, "Many times when the Lord gives direction, before the plan can be fulfilled, He calls us to a period of waiting. During this time, He refines our character. He also calls us to a time of prayer."[2] We are waiting for the Lord because He has told us to wait: *"Wait*

---

2. Keith Wright, sermon, Colonial Presbyterian Church, Kansas City, Missouri, January 28, 1996.

for the LORD; *be strong and take heart and wait for the* LORD" (Psalm 27:14). In Psalm 38:8–10, the psalmist expresses how very hard it is at times to wait to hear from the Lord:

> *I am feeble and utterly crushed; I groan in anguish of heart. All my longings lie open before you, Lord; my sighing is not hidden from you. My heart pounds, my strength fails me; even the light has gone from my eyes.*

But look at how he changes his mood in Psalm 38:15: "*I wait for you, O* LORD; *you will answer, Lord my God.*"

Abraham had to wait twenty-five years for God to fulfill His promise to make him a great nation, which is recorded in Genesis 12:2–3. When the promise was given, Abraham was seventy-five years old (Genesis 12:4). Sarah didn't deliver their promised child until she was ninety and Abraham was one hundred years old (Genesis 17:17 and 21:5). Jacob had to work for fourteen years to get Rachel for his wife (Genesis 29:18, 23–27).

Think of the Old Testament believers who didn't hear from the Lord for 400 years, and finally, the Messiah was born. We are able to hear the Lord by reading the Bible with the help of the Holy Spirit who lives within us. Those in the Old Testament only heard from the Lord through prophets through whom God spoke. I live every day rejuvenated because I am able to read God's Word. I cannot imagine not hearing from Him for one day, let alone not hearing from Him during my whole life.

There are lots of Scriptures to encourage us in our times of waiting for a certain direction from God:

- "*I wait for the* LORD, *my soul waits, and in his word I put my hope. My soul waits for the* LORD *more than watchmen wait for the morning, more than watchmen wait for the morning*" (Psalm 130:5–6).

- *"Wait for the LORD and keep his way. He will exalt you to inherit the land"* (Psalm 37:34).
- *"My sheep listen to my voice; I know them, and they follow me"* (John 10:27).

Over the years, I have had many people say that they have difficulty hearing God's direction, hearing His voice. Someone said that as we learn to hear God's voice, we don't have to worry about whether we are good at hearing. We can trust that He is good at speaking. I love that! Praise God! Of course that is true, and doesn't that lift a burden off your shoulders?

Plan of Action

1. What are you waiting for the Lord to provide? A healing? A resolved relationship? Direction for your next step? Take it to Him and trust that He will answer you in His time. Meanwhile, *"Cast all your anxiety on him because he cares for you"* (1 Peter 5:7).

2. While you wait, don't sit and do nothing. Look around. Where is God at work in your neighborhood or community or church? What opportunity sits before you? He has work for you to do while you wait. Perhaps what He has for you now is as important as that for which you are waiting. Remember while I waited for the Lord to arrest my chronic cough, He had me write *Books 1–3* of *Lord, It's Time for Just You and Me*. As you can see, He has me writing *Book 4*. All glory to Him!

Prayer

Lord, You are such a marvel! Fine-tune our ears to hear Your voice and then nudge us toward Your will. Help us to find great satisfaction in the center of Your will. Help us to find great joy as we serve You wherever You call us. Through us, bless and minister to others who need encouragement, wisdom, and Your love. Let us be exemplary ambassadors for You. Use us to draw others to You. These things are only possible in You. We leave these and all things with You. Work them out in Your way and in Your time. Thank You, Lord. I pray in Jesus' name. Amen.

TONGUES

Scripture Reading: James 3:1–12

"The tongue can bring death or life; those who love to talk will reap the consequences" (Proverbs 18:21 NLT).

"Words kill, words give life; they're either poison or fruit—you choose" (Proverbs 18:21 MSG).

Okay. Admit it. When you read the title, you figured I was going to discuss speaking in tongues as referred to in Acts 2:4. No, I am actually talking about the muscular organ that is in our mouths.

Have you ever really looked at your tongue? It is a very strange group of muscles, isn't it? Lately, after I brush my teeth, I brush my tongue over, under, and on both sides because some dentists encourage us to brush our tongues. It helps remove plaque and bacteria, which can cause bad breath. As I go through the motions of brushing my tongue, it seems to have a mind of its own. It doesn't always follow the directions my mind is giving it. I remember when the dentist had to put some gummy gooey stuff over my back molar to make a form for a crown; she had to ask me to move my tongue. Really? What was my tongue doing there?!

When the Bible speaks of the tongue, often it is referring to the use of the tongue to form words. As *The Message* says words can kill or they can give life. You've heard the saying "Sticks and stones may break my bones, but words will never hurt me." We know that is not true. We wish it were true, but it is not. Words can wound deeply. Scripture says that words are powerful. I read somewhere that we have to work against repeating in our minds and believing the ugly words that people have said to us. Instead, we need to fill our minds with what Scripture says to us. *"Fix your thoughts on what is true, and honorable, and right, and admirable. Think about things that are excellent and worthy of praise"* (Philippians 4:8 NLT).

How important are we to God, our Father? We are important enough that He gave His one and only Son to die in our place and to welcome us into His family. Let's look at Romans 5:8 *"But God demonstrates his own love for us in this: While we were still sinners, Christ died for us."* These are words we need to say repeatedly to ourselves rather than repeating mean and ugly words that have wounded us.

Plan of Action

1. Take time to look up other encouraging Scriptures with which you can fill your mind.

2. Ask the Lord to guard your tongue to keep it from speaking ugly words to anyone. When we use our tongue for good, we can give life to people. *"Kind words heal and help; cutting words wound and maim"* (Proverbs 15:4 MSG). Here is the same verse from *The Living Bible*: *"Gentle words cause life and health; griping brings discouragement."*

Prayer

Lord, as I remember ugly, mean words said to me, remind me to forgive the person who said them. Guard my heart and mind and help me not to dwell on wounding words or actions. Help me to dwell on the amazing fact that You love me and want the best for me. Guard my tongue that I don't wound others with it. Help me to bless others with it. I love You, Lord, and I pray in Jesus' name. Amen.

TRUST GOD'S GRACE

Scripture Reading: Matthew 28:16–20

"And God is able to make all grace abound to you, so that in all things at all times, having all that you need, you will abound in every good work"
(2 Corinthians 9:8).

When the subject arises concerning sharing God's work and His Word, I often hear people say that they're afraid to do this because they don't feel qualified. They believe they will say something wrong. Or they fear that questions will arise for which they will have no answer. Frankly, Satan loves this attitude! He deals in fear. But God does not. *"For God did not give us a spirit of timidity, but a spirit of power, of love and of self-discipline. So do not be ashamed to testify about our Lord"* (2 Timothy 1:7–8a). How's that for an encouraging Scripture?!

Now stop and read 2 Corinthians 9:8 quoted at the beginning of this page. Doesn't that Scripture bless your socks off?! God fills us with His grace. We can be sure that when we have an opportunity to speak of Him, He has arranged it, and He will give us whatever we need to tell others about Him. He created speech. He created you. He created me. Because of Christ, we have the

Holy Spirit living in us, and He can do the speaking for us. Can we trust the Holy Spirit to speak through us? The Scripture says His grace abounds *"so that in all things at all times, having all that [we] need, [we] will abound in every good work."* Jesus told us to make disciples (Matthew 28:19–20), and how will we do that if we don't tell people around us about our Lord?

As Christians we have the responsibility to immerse ourselves in His Word. We do our part to be prepared by studying His Word so that we are as equipped as possible to answer questions or give explanations. But beyond reading and studying daily, the rest is up to the Holy Spirit. Of course, our daily reading of the Bible helps us because the more of His Word we know, the more we know Him. Also the Lord instructs us in His Word to pray continually (1 Thessalonians 5:17). We can pray while we talk. Listen to Him and trust Him to give you the words that you need. Every person is different, and only God knows what it will take to touch each person to accept Him. As His ambassadors, our generous, loving God can certainly speak though us. Trust Him and tell your faith story.

Plan of Action

1. If you don't already have the habit of reading God's Word regularly, establish this habit. If you are using a Bible that is hard to understand, get a *Living Bible,* or *The New Living Translation,* or *The Message.* When I found out that the Bible was God's Word for me, I was in my early twenties. I started reading the *Living Bible* every morning before anyone else in my family was up. I was so captivated that I had to tear myself away to get ready for work. Find a time in your schedule to regularly read what God wants you to know. I recommend beginning with the book of Psalms in the Old Testament or with the Gospel of John in the New Testament. Using

devotionals such as this one can also be helpful. Read the Bible as God's letter to you, because it is.

2. If you haven't ever put your faith story down on paper, I recommend that you do. This will help you to have more confidence when you have an opportunity to share your story. Just be sure your faith story is more about Him and His work in you rather than emphasizing your previous "bad self."

3. Ask God to give you an opportunity to tell someone about Him and your faith story. Every time you tell it, you will gain more confidence. With each telling, the Lord may even give you new things you had forgotten in your life's story. Trust Him. He knows what the other person needs to hear. You are off to a new adventure! I am always in awe of what He says through me and the opportunities He gives me to tell others about Him. Don't be discouraged if you don't see a positive response to what you tell them. That's okay. It's your responsibility to tell others about Christ. It's God's responsibility to lift the veil and give them faith. *"For it is by grace you have been saved, through faith—and this not from yourselves, it is the gift of God—not by works, so that no one can boast"* (Ephesians 2:8–9).

Prayer

Lord, You know our fears about telling others about You and sharing our faith story. We know You do not give us fear. Only You know how to remove our insecurities and build our confidence and trust in You. We know that You want us to tell our friends and neighbors about Your love for them. We set ourselves before You and ask for Your strength, wisdom, and knowledge as we follow You in every part of our lives—even as we testify of Your glory and Your love for our friends and neighbors. We love You, and we pray in Jesus' name. Amen.

THE TRUTH

Scripture Reading: 1 Kings 17:1–24

"Now I know that you are a man of God and that the word of the LORD from your mouth is the truth" (1 Kings 17:24).

Nearly every morning I eat oatmeal for breakfast. I know how much oatmeal it takes to make a meal for me, just as I am sure the widow in chapter 17 of 1 Kings knew how much flour it would take to make bread for her and her son.

As the story went, she was planning to use the last of her flour and oil to make bread, *"that we may eat it—and die"* (1 Kings 17:12). She fully expected that bread would be their last meal, and they would then die of starvation.

However, along came Elijah, and he asked for some of the bread she planned to make for herself and her son. Elijah spoke God's word to her, *"The jar of flour will not be used up and the jug of oil will not run dry until the day the LORD gives rain on the land"* (1 Kings 17:14).

The Scripture records the fact that from that day on there was food every day for Elijah, the widow, and her son. God provided flour and oil when in reality, both should have been used up with the first meal she made for Elijah. Every day this widow witnessed the miracle of God's promise that neither her flour nor oil would run dry until rain appeared.

First Kings 17:17 tells us that *"some time later"* her son became ill and stopped breathing. Elijah took her son to the room where Elijah was staying and asked God to restore his life, which He did. The widow's response? *"Now I know that you are a man of God and that the word of the LORD from your mouth is the truth"* (1 Kings 17:24). Of course, she was undoubtedly overwhelmed and immeasurably grateful that God gave her back her son. And of course, when the boy's life was restored after Elijah asked God to give him life, she came face to face with the fact that Elijah was truly a man of God who spoke His truth. But hadn't she seen that in the nourishing provision that God had provided *"for some time"* (1 Kings 17:17)?

The widow's lack of understanding is not different from many others recorded in Scripture. Her lack of understanding is not different from ours. How many of us have witnessed lives snatched from death at the last minute? Was it a miraculous recovery from an illness, a miraculous delivery from a sure fatal accident, money supplied at just the right time, or some other amazingly supernatural happening? Though we have seen God's hand intervene on our behalf, we still react in fear when a new threat arises.

I praise God that He does not turn His back on us when we cower in fear at a new challenge. He is faithful to help us in our unbelief even though we should walk solidly in our faith based on His faithfulness to walk through the valley of the shadow of death with us (Psalm 23:4).

Plan of Action

1. Elijah was truly a man of God who spoke His truth. Let us look at the fruit of our leaders (Galatians 5:22–23). Do they speak the truth? Or are they confused at best or liars at worst (Luke 6:43–45)? Let's rely on the Holy Spirit to give us discernment.

2. We know truth by reading His Word, the Bible. As we do that, He changes us and helps us to discern truth from falsehood. The widow had Elijah physically with her. We have the Holy Spirit living in us and teaching us His Word (John 14:26). As we read God's Word, let's listen to and allow the Holy Spirit to teach us (2 Timothy 3:16–17).

Prayer

Father, we need Your help to identify poor leaders who are confused or even liars. Help us to identify, follow, and support good leaders who know You and Your truth for us. Draw us to Your choice of leaders. Please raise up good, honest, Christian leaders for our churches, our cities, and every other important place in our lives. Give us discernment as we read and hear "news reports." The reporters are human and often give their slant on the "news" they report. Rather than complain about things, move us to get involved and work with those good leaders. Please help us to stand strong with You wherever You take us. Let us be a blessing to You, our family, our church, and all the people You place in our path. We love You, Lord, and we pray in Jesus' name. Amen.

THE VEIL OF UNBELIEF

Scripture Reading: Matthew 27:45–54

"But their minds were hardened. For to this day, when they read the old covenant, that same veil remains unlifted, because only through Christ is it taken away"
(2 Corinthians 3:14 ESV).

I have a very sweet friend with whom I was discussing the process of publishing *Lord, It's Time for Just You and Me, Book 3*. After she heard several people talking about it, she said, "I will have to get a signed copy of it once it's published. I've heard so much about it." This friend had told me in the past that she didn't believe in God. I reminded her that my book is a Christian devotional, to which she replied, "I know. But I want to support you, and just reading your book won't convert me to believe in your God." She's absolutely correct! Until the Lord God, lifts the veil of unbelief (2 Corinthians 3:16–17), no one can become a Christian.

Do you remember in the Bible when it tells us about the hour when Jesus dying on the cross? Let's read the narrative as Luke describes it:

It was now about the sixth hour, and darkness came over the whole land until the ninth hour, for the sun stopped shining. And the curtain of the temple was torn in two. Jesus called out with a loud voice, "Father, into your hand I commit my spirit." When he had said this, he breathed his last.

—Luke 23:44–46

The temple curtain that was torn in two just before Jesus died is the curtain that separated the Holy of Holies from the rest of the temple. Matthew 27:51–53 gives a bit more information: "*At that moment the curtain of the temple was torn in two from the top to bottom. The earth shook and the rocks split.*" The temple curtain was torn from the top to the bottom by God. In this way and because of Christ's sacrifice, He allows His believers to come right into His presence. We don't have to rely on any other person to speak to God. We can ask Him questions directly. "*In him [Christ] and through faith in him we may approach God with freedom and confidence*" (Ephesians 3:12). Thank You, Lord!

Plan of Action

1. Take a few minutes to consider what your life would be like if you always had to rely on someone else to take your prayers to God. Aren't we eternally grateful that God changed that for us?

2. Spend another few minutes praising and thanking God that He has given us His Holy Spirit and His Word to teach, comfort, and encourage us. In His Word, we learn of His love for us.

Prayer

O, my precious Lord, I am so sorry You had to die on the cross in my place. What can I possibly say to let You know how very grateful I am? I know Your Word tells us that You don't want sacrifices. You want obedience instead. Then, Lord, please help me to forever be obedient whenever, wherever, and with whomever You lead me. I love You, Lord, and I am so privileged to be Your daughter. I pray in the beautiful name of Jesus. Amen.

WE WILL WORSHIP AT HIS FEET

Scripture Reading: John 13:1–17 and Philippians 2:5–11

*"Oh come, let us worship and bow down; let us kneel before the L*ORD*, our Maker"* (Psalm 95:6 ESV)!

"Let us go to his dwelling place, let us worship at his footstool" (Psalm 132:7).

My husband and I attend a wonderful, large church in southern Florida. We have five pastors who are great preachers, and we also have a great worship team that leads in singing praises to our Lord and helps to prepare us to hear God's Word. Even though the leaders of the church serve diligently to help us focus on God and what He wants to say to us, I occasionally find myself distracted by the people in front and even around me. I seriously wish that I could have a tube around my face that goes directly to the stage where the worship team is. With that I wouldn't be so easily distracted from worshiping God as we sing. I do know that God instructs us to worship and sing together. Psalm 95:1 tells us: *"Come, let us sing for joy to the L*ORD*; let us shout aloud to the Rock of our salvation."* Yes, we can worship alone, and we can worship together. I just need to learn not to be distracted by my sisters and brothers-in-Christ as I worship with them.

When I am at home listening to Christian music, I am able to maintain my focus and worship God. I am so grateful for the private time I have with Him. Even when I am writing, I am focused on Him because I want to write what He wants me to say. He cracks me up when He gives me words that I'm not familiar with. In fact, I check the meaning in the dictionary to be sure I am using each word correctly. He makes me sound much brighter than I am.

Have you ever considered that Christ who washed the disciples' feet now stands in power at the right side of our heavenly Father? Christ left His secure place in heaven, where He reigned with His Father, to come to this earth as a helpless baby, and He did that to save us from going to hell. He shed His blood and died on the cross in your place and in my place. He took upon His body the sins of the world—my sins, your sins. He did this so that our heavenly Father could have many children in heaven with Him. Those who have accepted Jesus' sacrifice of His body as their own sacrifice are blessed beyond measure as Jesus' brothers and sisters. I have no doubt that we will all worship at His feet when He returns.

The Apostle Paul wrote in Romans 14:11 quoting Isaiah 45:23, *"For it is written, 'As I live, says the Lord, every knee shall bow to Me, and every tongue confess to God'"* (NKJV). He wrote in Philippians 2:6–11 about Christ leaving His position in heaven and coming to the earth as a baby. Our Father was pleased with Christ for obediently allowing His body to be sacrificed for us:

> *Therefore, God elevated him to the place of highest honor and gave him the name above all other names, that at the name of Jesus every knee should bow, in*

heaven and on earth and under the earth, and every tongue confess that Jesus Christ is Lord, to the glory of God the Father.

—Philippians 2:9–11 NLT

On that day I won't be easily distracted.

Plan of Action

1. When I am at home and getting ready to go to our church service, I love playing Christian music. It helps me to focus on Him and His majesty. If you haven't tried this, you might want to. You can go to the Spotify App on your smartphone and ask it to play music by a specific group such as Casting Crowns or Mercy Me. The App is free.

2. You may not be familiar with all the ways we can worship our Lord. As the quoted Scriptures above state, we can worship on our knees. We can worship with raised hands (Psalm 134:2 and Nehemiah 8:6), by bowing (Exodus 12:27), by standing (Exodus 33:10), by singing (Psalm 33:3; Colossians 3:16), by praising Him (Psalm 42:5), by helping other people (Matthew 25:40), by memorizing His Word (Psalm 119:11), just to list a few ways found in the Bible. We need to remember that whatever we do, He is looking at our heart (1 Samuel 16:7). Are we doing what we are doing to worship and praise our Lord, or are we doing it for other people's reactions? God sees our heart:

   - *"Create in me a clean heart, O God, and renew a right spirit within me"* (Psalm 51:10 ESV).
   - *"Blessed are the pure in heart, for they shall see God"* (Matthew 5:8).
   - *"Search me, O God, and know my heart; test me and know my anxious thoughts. See if there is any offensive way in me, and lead me in the way everlasting"* (Psalm 139:23–24).

Prayer

Lord, teach me to worship You in Spirit and in truth. I know You are worthy of the highest praise. Lead me. Teach me. You have said that if we want wisdom, we can ask You, and You will answer us. Thank You that this is a desire of my heart, and thank You that You placed it there. I love You. I adore You. I praise You. In Jesus' name and to His glory. Amen.

WHAT WILL YOU SAY?

Scripture Reading: Luke 16:19–31

"Be wise in the way you act toward outsiders; make the most of every opportunity. Let your conversation be always full of grace, seasoned with salt, so that you may know how to answer everyone" (Colossians 4:5–6).

"But in your hearts set apart Christ as Lord. Always be prepared to give an answer to everyone who asks you to give the reason for the hope that you have. But do this with gentleness and respect" (1 Peter 3:15–16).

I have a very good friend who leads a diverse group of people who happen to have various faith traditions and even one of no faith, namely an atheist. My friend loves his job and respects each of the men and women of the different faiths.

One day, it occurred to me that he needed to be prepared for a time when one of his chaplains might come to him privately and ask him about Jesus and why he puts his faith in Him as a Christian. Isn't that what 1 Peter 3:15–16 says? All of us need to be prepared to give a reason for the hope we have to anyone whether they are aligned with another religion or no religion. Jesus said:

> *All authority in heaven and on earth has been given to me. Therefore go and make disciples of all nations, baptizing them in the name of the Father and of the Son and of the Holy Spirit teaching them to obey everything I have commanded you. And surely I am with you always, to the very end of the age.*
> —Matthew 28:18b–20

Did you catch the last part of Jesus' instruction? He ended it with a promise that wherever we go, whatever we do, and with whomever we talk, He is with us.

Now how about you? Are you prepared to give a reason for the hope you have? What if someone asked you to tell them why you have chosen to put your faith in Christ as Savior and Lord? Can you explain what that means? If you have not thought about how Christ wooed you to Himself, I recommend that you set your thoughts down in writing. If you have put your testimony in writing but it was many years ago, you might want to edit it a bit so you can include where God has you now. Be ready to warn them that after death, there are only two places we will go: heaven or hell. We will either go to heaven because we've accepted that Christ's death on the cross is the sacrifice for our sin, or we will go to hell because we ignored or denied Christ's death on the cross in our place.

On March 16, 2025, we had an English gentleman visit our Church in Southwestern Florida. He was a remarkable speaker whose name is Rico Tice. He has a ministry called "Hope Explored." He told of a time in his college years at Cambridge when a friend of his played a tape for a few of his fellow Rugby players. On this tape Rico spoke of his faith in Christ. After listening to the tape, Dave, one of Rico's fellow Rugby players, said, "Rico's not my friend." The other rugby players said, "Oh come on, Dave. Rico is one of your best friends." Dave replied, "We've played rugby together for eighteen months, and he's never told me about his faith in Jesus. If we were such good friends, wouldn't he have told me about such an important part of his life?"

What about us? Do we have friends with whom we have not shared our faith in Christ?" When they hear of salvation through Christ's life, death, and resurrection, will they think sadly or angrily of you because you never spoke of your faith to them?

Plan of Action

1. Take a moment. Do you have any friends whom you have not told of Christ's sacrifice on their behalf?

2. I love how Rico suggested we begin the conversation. "We have been friends for many years (or for two years, whatever is apropos) and I would not be a very good friend if I didn't ask you, 'What do you think of Christ?'" Depending on your friend's answer, you may need to tell him your testimony or explain that if he thinks he will get to heaven because he is *good enough*, then why in the world would have our loving God sent His only Son to die in our place. God is perfect. God is love. But God will not overlook someone ignoring the death of His precious Son as a sacrifice for us.

Prayer

Lord, please remind me of friends with whom I have not shared the good news of Christ as Savior and Lord. Prepare me for each individual conversation. I know that You both precede me and follow me and lay Your hand of blessing on my head (Psalm 139:5), and I thank You for that. I trust that You will prepare me for each response and help me to give a sound, understandable, and penetrating answer for the hope I have in Christ. I also thank You that You love my friends even more than I do. Let me walk in Your wisdom and let the good news easily come from my mouth as I speak with those You have in my life. I pray in the mighty name of Jesus. Amen.

WIELD YOUR SWORD

Scripture Reading: Psalm 119:1–16

"I have hidden your word in my heart that I might not sin against you" (Psalm 119:11).

"For the word of God is living and active. Sharper than any double-edged sword, it penetrates even to dividing soul and spirit, joints and marrow; it judges the thoughts and attitudes of the heart" (Hebrews 4:12).

Many years ago, in fact decades ago, I had finished reading *The Hiding Place* by Corrie ten Boom with Elizabeth and John Sherrill. If you have not read this book, I highly recommend it. She strongly encouraged her readers to memorize Scripture because there might be a time when we don't have our Bibles within reach. Because of her book and her encouragement, I decided that I wanted to memorize Scripture. On this particular day, the Scripture given in my daily

Bible reading is Isaiah 43:2–3. I was using *The Revised Standard Version* of the Bible, which says:

> *When you pass through the waters I will be with you; and through the rivers, they shall not overwhelm you; when you walk through fire you shall not be burned, and the flame shall not consume you. For I am the LORD your God.*

First of all, isn't that an amazing promise?!! I was so moved when I read that Scripture that I immediately asked God to help me to memorize it. As a former French teacher, I remembered that my students could recite the French songs quicker than they could recite the dialogues they had to memorize. Thus I asked God to give me music to go along with those verses. And of course, our generous, gracious, loving God did that. Over the years He has blessed me with many other melodies to help me memorize His Word.

Now to my point, a few months ago, I became very ill to the point I couldn't even lift my phone. This lasted for three days. Finally on the last day, I remembered Proverbs 3:1 where God tells us *"do not forget my teaching, but keep my commands in your heart, for they will prolong your life many years."* Then later in the same chapter, *"This will bring health to your body and nourishment to your bones"* (Proverbs 3:8). With that I searched my groggy mind and pulled up Psalm 27 verse 1: *"The Lord is my light and my salvation whom shall I fear"* (TLB)? I must let you know that I was not thinking of a human being that I feared. I was safe in our daughter's home. I love our daughter and our son-in-law, and I know they love me. When I look back on that time, it seems that the Scripture that I could recall had nothing to do with my being ill. I just know that once I started focusing my mind on His Word, I began to distance myself from the horrible sickness.

Until that illness I couldn't imagine a time when I couldn't place my hands on a Bible. I certainly never thought of being so ill that I hated to move my body. I praise God for healing me. Perhaps if I had brought Scripture to mind, my illness wouldn't have lasted three days. I hope I am never that sick again to find out.

Plan of Action

1. Corrie ten Boom, and now even Cheryl Lynn Betz, says it is important to memorize God's Word. We never know when the time may come that we can't put our hands on a Bible. God made us all different, and because of that He knows the best method for us to memorize His Word. For me it was with music. Ask Him what method is best for you.

2. You will find once you have memorized His Word that you will have many opportunities to bring it up in everyday conversations, both with Christian friends and even with non-Christian friends. Let the Holy Spirit nudge you, and then say it just like you would discuss the weather—calmly, kindly. I look at this as adding flowers to a conversation. Of course, it is much more powerful than flowers.

3. When I send birthday, anniversary, and get well cards, I either write an appropriate Scripture in the card, or I pick a card that already has Scripture printed on it. I remember when my father died, the cards with Scripture ministered more deeply to my grief than those that had just a kind sentiment.

Prayer

Lord, You know and love every person who is reading this prayer. Move them to memorize Your Word, and then Lord, give them opportunities to speak the verse in a conversation or write it in a note to someone. Thank You for loving us. We love You and pray in Jesus' name. Amen.

APPENDIX I

Steps to Salvation with Scriptures

Romans 3:23 "All have sinned and fall short of the glory of God."

Romans 5:8 "But God demonstrates his own love for us in this: While we were still sinners, Christ died for us."

1 John 1:9 "If we confess our sins, he is faithful and just and will forgive us our sins and purify us from all unrighteousness."

John 3:16 "For God so loved the world that he gave his one and only Son, that whoever believes in him shall not perish but have eternal life."

Romans 10:9 "If you confess with your mouth, 'Jesus is Lord,' and believe in your heart that God raised him from the dead, you will be saved."

John 1:12 "Yet to all who received him, to those who believed in his name, he gave the right to become children of God."

Philippians 1:6 "Being confident of this, that he who began a good work in you will carry it on to completion until the day of Christ Jesus."

Three Questions to Ask When Introducing Someone to Christ

These are taken from Leith Samuel from Southampton, England and are quoted and expounded upon in Paul E. Little's book *How to Give Away Your Faith* on pages 84 and 85.

1. "Have you ever personally trusted Jesus Christ or are you still on the way?" Then you listen to the person's answer.

2. "That's interesting. How far along the way are you?" Be hypersensitive to the condition of the person with whom you are speaking. This is the time when they may bring up the faith of their grandmother, or how the Lord has been leading them lately, or any number of things, which may seem out of context. Listen, and ask the Holy Spirit to guide you along.

3. "Would you like to become a real Christian and be sure of it?"

This would be a good time to take them through the scriptures above.

APPENDIX II

Step-by-Step Scriptures

He guides me in paths of righteousness for his name's sake.

(Psalm 23:3)

Show me your ways, O LORD, teach me your paths; guide me in your truth and teach me, for you are God my Savior, and my hope is in you all day long.

(Psalm 25:4–5)

Show me the path where I should go, O Lord; point out the right road for me to walk. Lead me; teach me; for you are the God who gives me salvation. I have no hope except in you.

(Psalm 25:4–5 TLB)

He guides the humble in what is right and teaches them his way.

(Psalm 25:9)

The Lord is good and glad to teach the proper path to all who go astray; he will teach the ways that are right and best to those who humbly turn to him. And when we obey him, every path he guides us on is fragrant with his lovingkindness and his truth.

(Psalms 25:8–10 TLB)

I will instruct you and teach you in the way you should go; I will counsel you and watch over you.

(Psalm 32:8)

I will instruct you [says the Lord] *and guide you along the best pathway for your life; I will advise you and watch your progress.*

(Psalm 32:8 TLB)

Taste and see that the LORD is good; blessed is the man who takes refuge in him . . . The lions may grow weak and hungry, but those who seek the Lord lack no good thing.

(Psalm 34:8, 10)

If the Lord delights in a man's way, he makes his steps firm; though he stumble, he will not fall, for the Lord upholds him with his hand.

(Psalm 37:23–24)

The steps of good men are directed by the Lord. He delights in each step they take.

(Psalm 37:23 TLB)

For this God is our God for ever and ever; he will be our guide even to the end.

(Psalm 48:14)

In God I trust; I will not be afraid, what can man do to me? . . . For you have delivered me from death and my feet from stumbling, that I may walk before God in the light of life.

(Psalm 56:11, 13)

Let everyone bless God and sing his praises, for he holds our lives in his hands. And he holds our feet to the path.

(Psalm 66:8 TLB)

Blessed are those whose strength is in you, who have set their hearts on pilgrimage. . .. They go from strength to strength, till each appears before God in Zion.

(Psalm 84:5, 7)

Happy are those who are strong in the Lord, who want above all else to follow your steps. . .. They will grow constantly in strength and each of them is invited to meet with the Lord in Zion.

(Psalm 84:5, 7 TLB)

Teach me your way, O Lord, and I will walk in your truth; give me an undivided heart that I may fear your name.

(Psalm 86:11)

Tell me where you want me to go and I will go there. May every fiber of my being unite in reverence to your name.

(Psalm 86:11 TLB)

The Lord will keep you from all harm—he will watch over your life; the Lord will watch over your coming and going both now and forevermore.

(Psalm 121:7–8)

He keeps you from all evil, and preserves your life. He keeps his eye upon you as you come and go, and always guards you.

(Psalm 121:7–8 TLB)

You hem me in—behind and before; you have laid your hand upon me.

(Psalm 139:5)

You both precede and follow me, and place your hand of blessing on my head.

(Psalm 139:5 TLB)

Let the morning bring me word of your unfailing love, for I have put my trust in you. Show me the way I should go, for to you I lift up my soul.

(Psalm 143:8)

Let me see your kindness to me in the morning, for I am trusting you. Show me where to walk, for my prayer is sincere.
(Psalm 143:8 TLB)

In his heart a man plans his course, but the Lord determines his steps.

(Proverbs 16:9)

We should make plans—counting on God to direct us.

(Proverbs 16:9 TLB)

A man's steps are directed by the Lord.

(Proverbs 20:24)

They that wait upon the Lord shall renew their strength. They shall mount up with wings like eagles; they shall run and not be weary; they shall walk and not faint.

(Isaiah 40:31 TLB)

Fear not, for I am with you. Do not be dismayed. I am your God. I will strengthen you; I will help you; I will uphold you with my victorious right hand.

(Isaiah 41:10 TLB)

The Lord will guide you always; he will satisfy your needs in a sun-scorched land and will strengthen your frame. You will be like a well-watered garden, like a spring whose waters never fail.

(Isaiah 58:11)

I know, O Lord, that a man's life is not his own; it is not for man to direct his steps.

(Jeremiah 10:23)

When Jesus spoke again to the people, he said, "I am the light of the world. Whoever follows me will never walk in darkness, but will have the light of life."

(John 8:12)

Jesus answered, "I am the way and the truth and the life. No one comes to the Father except through me."

(John 14:6)

Faith comes from hearing the message, and the message is heard through the word of Christ.

(Romans 10:17)

No temptation has seized you except what is common to man. And God is faithful; he will not let you be tempted beyond what you can bear. But when you are tempted, he will also provide a way out so that you can stand up under it.

(1 Corinthians 10:13)

Since we live by the Spirit, let us keep in step with the Spirit.

(Galatians 5:25)

If any of you lacks wisdom, he should ask God, who gives generously to all without finding fault, and it will be given to him.

(James 1:5)

But if we walk in the light, as he is in the light, we have fellowship with one another, and the blood of Jesus, his Son, purifies us from all sin.

(1 John 1:7)

It has given me great joy to find some of your children walking in the truth, just as the Father commanded us.

(2 John 4)

APPENDIX III

Scriptures Referenced in the Devotional, excluding the Appendixes

Scripture Reference—*Devotional*

Genesis
1:3—*The Son Is Invading My Shade*
1:20–28—*God's Word—Truth*
1:27—*The Majesty of God*
3:17—*Thorns and Thistles*
3:18—*Thorns and Thistles*
12:2–4—*A Time to Wait*
17:17—*A Time to Wait*
21:5—*A Time to Wait*
29:18—*A Time to Wait*
29:23–27—*A Time to Wait*

Exodus
1:7—*Clueless but Teachable*
1:1–12:30—*Clueless but Teachable*
3:1–14—*Egypt After the Exodus*
12—*The Lamb of God*
12:3–13—*Clueless but Teachable*
12:7—*We Will Worship at His Feet*
12:30—*Clueless but Teachable*
12:31–32—*Clueless but Teachable*
12:36—*Clueless but Teachable*
12:37–38—*Clueless but Teachable*
12:40—*Clueless but Teachable*
14:5—*Clueless but Teachable*
15:11—*The Majesty of God*
19:5—*The Proud Father*
29:38–43—*The Lamb of God*
33:10—*We Will Worship at His Feet*

Numbers
22:21–39—*Jonah*
28:1–10—*The Lamb of God*

Deuteronomy
5:21—*Covet—You Shall Not; Jealousy*
10:12–13—*Fear*
31:6—*The Proud Father; The Rich Man; The Son Is Invading My Shade*
31:8—*His Many Blessings; Reflection*

Joshua
1:5—*The Son Is Invading My Shade*
2—*A Time to Wait*
3:15, 16—*Fear*
7:26—*I Am a Sinner, Forgiven*

1 Samuel
3—*Jonah*
3:1–10—*On Call; Seize the Idea!*
15:22b—*The Proud Father*
16:7b—*Change; Feigned Interest*
16:7— *We Will Worship at His Feet*
18:1–4—*Make the Call*

2 Samuel
2:28—*Thorns and Thistles*

1 Kings
17:1–24—*The Truth*
18:1—*A Time to Wait*

2 Kings
5:1–16—*God Healed Me*

1 Chronicles
28:20—*The Son Is Invading My Shade*
29:11—*The Majesty of God*

2 Chronicles
26:1–21—*The Parable of the Rich Farmer*
26:5b—*The Parable of the Rich Farmer*

Nehemiah
8:6—*We Will Worship at His Feet*

Job
38–41—*Jellybeans*

Psalms
8:9—*The Majesty of God*
16:7—*Seize the Idea*
23:4—*The Truth*
24:1–2—*God, Our Creator; God's Word—Truth*
27:1–3—*Fear*
27:1—*Wield Your Sword*
27:3—*The Storm*
27:14—*A Time to Wait*

30:2—God Healed Me; God Healed My Husband
32:8—Clueless but Teachable; The Parable of the Rich Farmer
32:8–11—Seize the Idea
33:3—We Will Worship at His Feet
37:34—A Time to Wait
38:8–10—A Time to Wait
38:15—A Time to Wait
42:5— We Will Worship at His Feet
51:10—We Will Worship at His Feet
66:20— Conversations with God
71:1–2—The Storm
75:6–7—Jealousy
90:12—God Is Not Done . . .
90:17— His Many Blessings
91:1—We Will Worship at His Feet
95:6—We Will Worship at His Feet
101:3—Resist the Devil
101:4—Resist the Devil
103:2–3—God Healed My Husband
104:1—The Majesty of God
105:23–45—Clueless but Teachable
118—Be thankful
118:1—Be Thankful
119—Clueless but Teachable
119:1–16—Wield Your Sword
119:11— We Will Worship at His Feet; Wield Your Sword
127:3–5—God's Word—Truth
130:5–6—A Time to Wait
132:7—We Will Worship at His Feet
134:2—We Will Worship at His Feet
138—Be Thankful
138:7—Fear; The Storm
138:8—The Lamb of God; The Proud Father; The Son Is Invading My Shade
139:1–18, 23–24—The Proud Father
139:5—Be Thankful; Fear; What Will You Say?
139:7–12—Jonah
139:13—Be Thankful; Reflection
139:14—Comparison; Reflection
139:16—Jesus Is Saving a Seat for You
139:23–24— I Am a Sinner, Forgiven; The Son Is Invading My Shade
145:5—The Majesty of God
145:8–9—Jonah

Proverbs
3:1—*Wield Your Sword*
3:8—*Wield Your Sword*
3:20, 22—*God's Word—Truth*
8:17—*A God Appointment*
10:20—*Our Risen Lord*
14:30—*Comparison*
15:4—*Tongues*
16:24—*Make the Call*
16:28—*Thorns and Thistles*
18:21—*Thorns and Thistles; Tongues*
31:10–31—*Mother*

Isaiah
6:8—*On Call*
37:16—*God, Our Creator; God's Word—Truth*
40:10—*Fear*
43:1—*Perspective*
43:2–3—*Wield Your Sword*
45:9, 11–12—*Jealousy*
45:18–25—*God, Our Creator*
45:23—*We Will Worship at His Feet*
48:17—*An Influencer*
53:1–12—*God Healed Me*
53:7–8—*A God Appointment*
55:10–11—*Be Prepared*

Jeremiah
29:11—*Comparison; God Is Not Done . . . ; His Many Blessings; An Influencer; Jealousy*
33:3—*Conversations with God; Seize the Idea*

Lamentations
3:22–23—*Reflection*

Jonah
1:1–4:11—*Jonah*

Zephaniah
3:17—*Conversations with God*

Matthew
3:16–17—*The Proud Father*
4:1–10—*Resist the Devil*
5:8—*We Will Worship at His Feet*
5:13–16—*Covet—You Shall Not*
5:27–28—*Resist the Devil*
6:8—*His Many Blessings*
6:25–34—*God, Our Creator*
7:1–5—*Judging*
7:7—*Jellybeans; The Lamb of God*
7:7–8—*God, Our Creator; Seize the Idea!*
7:7–11—*Jellybeans*

Appendix III

11:15—*Seize the Idea!*
13:1–23—*Scattering Seed*
14:22–32—*The Storm*
14:33—*The Storm*
16:21—*The Stone Had Been Rolled Away*
18:21–22—*I Am a Sinner, Forgiven*
20:1–16—*Comparison*
23:37–39—*Change*
25:40—*We Will Worship at His Feet*
27:45–54—*The Veil of Unbelief*
27:62–66—*The Stone Had Been Rolled Away*
28:1–10—*The Stone Had Been Rolled Away*
28:2—*Our Risen Lord*
28:3–4—*Our Risen Lord*
28:16–20—*Trust God's Grace*
28:18–20—*Fear; What Will You Say?*
28:19–20—*God's Word—Truth*

Mark

4:26–29—*Scattering Seed*
4:35–41—*The Storm*
5:1–20—*I Am a Sinner, Forgiven*
10:17–31—*The Rich Man*
16:1–7—*Peter*
16:15–16—*An Influencer*

Luke

3:23—*The Proud Father*
6:43–45—*The Truth*
8:40–48—*A Time to Wait*
9:37–43—*The Majesty of God*
12:6–7—*God, Our Creator*
12:13–21—*The Parable of the Rich Farmer*
16:19–31—*What Will You Say?*
17:11–19—*Dropping Pansies; His Many Blessings*
18:1–8—*God Healed Me*
18:9–14—*Conversations with God*
19:1–10—*Be Prepared*
19:28–40—*The Stone Had Been Rolled Away*
22:54–62—*Peter*
23:44–46—*The Veil of Unbelief*
24:1–50—*Our Risen Lord*

John

1:12—*The Proud Father*
1:29—*The Lamb of God*
3—*Perspective*
3:3—*Be Prepared; Lazarus, Come Out!*
3:3–8—*Perspective*
3:16—*Be Thankful; Comparison; Life Preserver; The Proud Father; Reflection*
5—*God Healed Me*

10:27—*A Time to Wait*
11:5—*Lazarus, Come Out!*
11:17–44—*Lazarus, Come Out!*
11:25–26—*Life Preserver*
13:1–17—*We Will Worship at His Feet*
13:34–35—*Feigned Interest*
14:1–7—*Jesus Is Saving a Seat for You*
14:15–17—*I Am a Sinner, Forgiven*
14:15–31—*Conversations with God*
14:16–17— *Conversations with God; Perspective*
14:20— *Conversations with God*
14:21—*The Proud Father*
14:26—*Life Preserver; Our Risen Lord; The Truth*
15:4–9—*God, Our Creator*
15:4–11—*Abide in Me*
20:1–18—*Our Risen Lord*
20:3–9—*Our Risen Lord*
20:15–16—*Our Risen Lord*
20:19—*The Stone Had Been Rolled Away*
20:19-23—*Our Risen Lord*
20:25—*Our Risen Lord*
20:26—*Our Risen Lord; The Stone Had Been Rolled Away*
20:30—*Our Risen Lord*
21—*Our Risen Lord*

Acts
2:4—*Tongues*
4:24—*God, Our Creator*
8:4—*Change*
8:26-40—*A God Appointment*
9:1-18—*Jonah*
9:1-22—*Our New Life*
9:32-43—*God Healed My Husband*
10—*Change*
10:1-23—*Jonah*
17:25b—*Be Thankful*
17:26—*Change; Comparison; Covet—You Shall Not; A God Appointment*

Romans
3:23—*Peter; The Proud Father*
5:5b—*Feigned Interest; Mother*
5:1-8—*I Am a Sinner, Forgiven*
5:8— *I Am a Sinner, Forgiven; The Proud Father; The Storm; Tongues*
6:23—*Be Prepared; An Influencer*
8:28—*Be Thankful; Comparison; God Is Not Done . . .; A Time to Wait; Mother*
8:29—*A God Appointment*
10:9—*The Proud Father*
12:2— *I Am a Sinner, Forgiven; Our New Life*

12:3—*Thorns and Thistles*
12:4-8—*Comparison*
12:6-8—*Church Members and Church Participants*
12:10—*Church Members and Church Participants*
14:11—*We Will Worship at His Feet*

1 Corinthians

6:19— *Conversations with God*
10:13— *I Am a Sinner, Forgiven; Resist the Devil*
10:31—*Dropping Pansies; The Parable of the Rich Farmer*
12—*Dropping Pansies*
12:4-7—*The Proud Father*
12:4-31—*Covet—You Shall Not*
13:4-7—*James*
4:1-11, 28—*Church Members and Church Participants*
13:12—*Abide in Me; I Am a Sinner, Forgiven; Seize the Idea!*
15:3-6—*Our Risen Lord*
16:14—*James*

2 Corinthians

3:14—*Scattering Seed; The Veil of Unbelief*
3:16-17—*The Veil of Unbelief*
3:17-18—*Our New Life*
3:18—*The Majesty of God; Mirrors*
5:17— *I Am a Sinner, Forgiven; Our New Life; Resist the Devil*
5:20—*A God Appointment*
9:8—*Trust God's Grace*

Galatians

1:10—*Comparison*
2:20—*Be Prepared*
5:22-23—*Mother; The Truth; Thorns and Thistles*
6:4-5—*Comparison*

Ephesians

1:13—*Our New Life*
1:17—*Jellybeans*
1:18-22—*Jellybeans*
2:8—*Trust God's Grace*
2:10—*God Is Not Done . . .*
3:12—*The Veil of Unbelief*
3:14-19—*Reflection*
3:20—*Scattering Seed*
4:1—*The Son Is Invading My Shade*
4:11-12—*Church Members and Church Participants*
4:22-24—*Mirrors; The Son Is Invading My Shade*
6:18—*Conversations with God*

Philippians
1:6—*Be Thankful; Mirrors*
1:17b—*God Is Not Done . . .*
1:25—*God Is Not Done . . .*
2:3-4—*Thorns and Thistles*
2:5-11—*We Will Worship at His Feet*
2:13—*Our New Life; The Rich Man The Son Is Invading My Shade*
4:6— *Conversations with God*
4:8—*Tongues*
4:19—*Comparison*

Colossians
1:6—*The Rich Man*
1:16-17—*God, Our Creator*
3:12—*The Proud Father*
3:12, 14—*James*
3:16— *We Will Worship at His Feet*
   3:15-17—*Be Thankful*
   4:5-6—*What Will You Say?*

1 Thessalonians
1:4—*The Majesty of God; Reflection*
5:16-18—*Jellybeans*
5:17—*Conversations with God; Trust God's Grace*

2 Timothy
1:6—*Covet—You Shall Not; Lazarus, Come Out!; The Proud Father*
1:7-8a—*Trust God's Grace*
2:15—*Clueless but Teachable*
3:14-17—*God's Word—Truth*
3:16-17—*Be Thankful; I Am Sinner, Forgiven; Perspective; The Truth*
4:2—*Scattering Seed*

Hebrews
1:3—*The Majesty of God*
4:12—*Wield Your Sword*
4:16— *Conversations with God*
5:11-6:8—*Thorns and Thistles*
1:7— *His Many Blessings*
6:7-8—*Thorns and Thistles*
12:1-11—*The Son Is Invading My Shade*
13:5— *I Am a Sinner, Forgiven*

James
1:5—*On Call*
1:17— *Clueless but Teachable; Covet—You Shall Not*
1:19—*Our Risen Lord*
2:1-4—*Jennie*
3:1—*Clueless but Teachable*
3:1-12—*Tongues*
4:3—*Jellybeans*
4:7—*Resist the Devil*

1 Peter

2:24—*God Healed Me*
3:15—*Be Prepared; Jonah*
3:15-16—*What Will You Say?*
5:7—*A Time to Wait*

2 Peter

1:16-17—*The Majesty of God*

1 John

1:9—*Our New Life; Peter*
3:1—*A God Appointment; Reflection*
4:4—*The Storm*

Revelation

5:13—*The Majesty of God*
12:10—*Resist the Devil*
20:12—*An Influencer*
22:3-4—*I Am a Sinner, Forgiven*

ONE LAST NOTE FROM THE AUTHOR

My Dear Reader,

If you have been blessed while reading this devotional, you may want to get my first book, *Lord, It's Time for Just You and Me*. You may email me at cbonmtn@aol.com to order it.

Or you may want to buy my second and third books: *Lord, It's Time for Just You and Me, Book 2*, and *Lord, It's Time for Just You and Me, Book 3* which you can find at www.amazon.com.

I do pray that God has used your reading of *Lord, It's Time for Just You and Me, Book 4* to draw you closer to Him. Let's glorify Him and enjoy Him together!

Blessings and Love in Christ,
Cheryl Lynn Betz

www.ingramcontent.com/pod-product-compliance
Lightning Source LLC
Chambersburg PA
CBHW080535170426
43195CB00016B/2565